FREEDOM FROM FEAR:

ON THE RECORD ABOUT COVID HYSTERIA, GOD, FASCISM AND THE WEST

MICHAEL J. SUTTON

HIDDEN ROAD PUBLISHING

Copyright © 2024 Michael J. Sutton

All rights reserved.

ISBN: 978-0-9756318-0-5

All rights reserved. No part of this book may be reproduced, stored in a retrieval system, or transmitted in any form or by any means, including electronic, mechanical, photocopy, recording, or otherwise, without the publisher's prior permission.

Unless noted, scriptures are taken from the Holy Bible, New International Version®, NIV®. Copyright © 1973, 1978, 1984, 2011 by Biblica, Inc.™ Used by permission of Zondervan. All rights reserved worldwide. www.zondervan.com The "NIV" and "New International Version" are trademarks registered in the United States Patent and Trademark Office by Biblica, Inc.™

Hidden Road Publishing

Other books by Michael J. Sutton:

Freedom from Fascism, a Christian Response to Mass Formation Psychosis
Is God on America's Side?
Is Russia Our Enemy?
Following Jesus when the Church has lost its Way.
The Third Tsunami
Monkey and the Castle by the Sea
The Curse of Crooked River
Baby Race
What are God's Pronouns?
The Lies, Legacies, and Lessons of Covid Hysteria

DEDICATION

No book is written in a vacuum. Ours is a world that is beset by war, conflict, fear, despair, fascism, tyranny, forgetfulness, and propaganda. At the end of last year, the world lost John Pilger, who was a famous journalist and filmmaker who challenged the narratives and was a thorn in the side of the political establishment in Australia, Britain, and America, where loyalty tests are the norm, and people sell their soul by turning their faces away and closing their eyes to the suffering of others.

But God sees everything, and I wonder what he thinks about it all, as each generation is called to stand up for truth and speak on the record to power, or about power, both secular and religious. Some of these encounters are recorded for us in the New Testament, to remind us that our earthly citizenship does not forfeit our responsibility to stand up for truth. We remember John Pilger, because he was an Australian, but we don't know the names of the hundred or so journalists killed in Gaza these last few months, nor the names of countless others, the victims of our political world of expediency. This is to our shame. This book is dedicated to the many journalists, activists, and individuals who have suffered during Covid Hysteria, the pogroms against Palestine, the cancel-culture, the propaganda war, loyalty tests, and warmongering, from both sides of the political divide, for there is the Left, and the Right, and then there is the truth.

CONTENTS

	Acknowledgments	i
1	Looking for the Authentic Jesus	1
2	16 May, 2023	20
3	18 May, 2023	49
4	9 June, 2023	71
5	11 August, 2023	92
6	25 September, 2023	114
7	1 October, 2023	139
8	7 October, 2023	176
9	27 October, 2023	210
10	28 November, 2023	232
11	19 December, 2023	251
12	22 December, 2023	293

ACKNOWLEDGMENTS

This is an interesting publication and reflects the spirit of the age. The printed word has been replaced by social media, blogs, and online opinion, a sea of words that are easily said, hastily written, and carelessly tossed aside. Most of what people say online is forgotten, deleted, or forms part of long email threads, or unread posts. Few have taken the time to publish what they write or edit or collate their words and their writings.

I decided to publish my 11 interviews from 2023 because what we say matters, and how we say it matters, and what we say needs to be remembered in this world of forgetfulness. These are my first interviews, and they are a distillation of my views on Covid Hysteria, fascism, the church, Covid Theology, Russia and Ukraine, America, Gaza, and Israel, among other issues. Radio and online interviews are very different from the written text. They have gaps, pauses, stops and starts, interjections, interruptions, incomplete sentences and phrases, and mistakes. Not all is negative however, as interviews can, in the heat of the moment, the stress of a difficult or pointed question, or out of the blue, produce remarkable, inspiring, memorable words, speeches and oratories.

It is an honor for someone to invite you onto their program to hear your views, or discuss your point of view, or listen to your perspective. It is like being invited into someone's home, and one is quickly aware of the furnishings, the style, the priorities, the books on the shelf, the atmosphere, and the temperature, and whether one is welcome or not. Like every home, every interviewer is different, and this reflects the richness of our society today, that even amongst the critics of the narrative, there is diversity. This diversity is a blessing, for it reminds me that the battle we fight today is not simply a spiritual or a political one, but it is deeply personal, whether to preserve these individual, diverse views, or force a sterile, conformist, sameness in the way the mainstream news has gone, a clone army of copies, a cut and paste industry, a replicated form, or an orchestrated message. Thank God for diversity, and the freedom, while it lasts, to stand for truth against secular and religious power in these controversial days.

None of the transcripts recorded here are official, nor did I ask permission from anyone, nor do I need to. They are unauthorized, and I went through and edited them myself, and tried to convey the original meaning. In the editing process, I tried to polish the words without changing their meaning, and some sentences had to be reconstructed because of their vagueness or other similar problems. My words are my words, and I own them, and have the right to place them in the context in which they have been spoken. All mistakes are my own and no doubt there will be some.

I was privileged to have been interviewed by four men whom I deeply respect, for their professionalism, their questions, and their ability to communicate effectively online which is the new world of communication. These men are Hrvoje Moric, Neil Johnson, Vic Dalziel, and Reuben Rose. If even 1% of the online world had men like these, the internet would be a different place.

This book is also important because it represents and collects some important reflections and concepts of Freedom Matters Today in its inception, or early years, 2021-3. As I have argued consistently, the Christian church has lost its way in the West, it is a toxic and corrupt institution, and is more concerned with reputation, investment, power, and money than the identity, the words, and the actions of Jesus.

But, there is a deeper critique, and that is 'going to church' is not essential for a Christian, but following Jesus is, and my critique has focused on the former rather than the latter, and I feel a conviction, a calling, and a commitment to talk more about what it means to follow Jesus, and leave the institutions which claim to represent God on earth, to God, for him to do what he likes with them. As for me, like John Wesley, George Whitfield, and Uchimura Kanzo, I am going outside the walls, beyond the monastery, and into the world where people are, to renew my personal understanding of a real Jesus, the man of authenticity, and the one who was the presence, the power, and the person of God among us.

I am not interested in reforming the church, for all reformation movements fail, and I am not interested in trying to save the church, for I can save no one, and I am not interested in defending the church, as history speaks for itself. More and more people are asking me about Jesus, who he is, who he was, and why he matters, and this is the true gospel, the true good news of the Christian faith, not bricks and mortar, not creeds and sects, not flags and pogroms, but Jesus of Nazareth who calls us all to follow him, because we all matter to God.

I would also like to thank the steadfast support of my mother, and the love and encouragement of my partner, Tatiana, who saw 'great words' in my writings against fascism and enabled me to find and express my voice. If it were not for her, Freedom Matters Today would have remained an idea, and she, perhaps more than anyone, truly understood what I was trying to do, and she truly understood the freedom I was trying to promote. This book is for her.

1

LOOKING FOR THE AUTHENTIC JESUS

It seems to me that one of the most significant inadequacies of today is the absence of authenticity. It is easy to go to the local supermarket and find cheap imitations of basic white goods, made from defective materials, in nice shiny boxes that last longer than what is enclosed. It is easy to go to the local restaurant quarter and find imitation Japanese restaurants which use frozen, imported salmon, and hard, stale rice, where every dish has the same slimy sauce, and everything is dosed with that secret oriental spice we know as MSG. Microwave ovens and restaurants even in this awful state are often more authentic than many people today, where authenticity is more likely to be misunderstood as a new clothes brand, than a trait of human character.

Everything seems fake today, from food, to news, to people, to smiles, to handshakes. We embrace with one eye on the clock and our minds elsewhere, we view friendship as a way to climb the social ladder, and charity as the path to personal gain. A few years ago, the former President of America, Donald Trump gained notoriety for speaking out aloud what we all knew to be true, the reality of fake news. He was roundly condemned by those on the Left and on the Right, though the idea of *'manufactured'* news, curated truth, and altered facts has been around for decades. The entire news editing process is one of selectivity, bias, and rush-to-the-bottom journalism. Nothing new to see here. Few journalists could say that they go to work for one of the large media groupings with a sincere interest in the truth with a straight face. It is about money, advertising, marketing, demographics and the bottom-line. Only when they are forced to by material interests, will these leviathans move in the right direction.

Ironically, the most severe critique of mass media in the past came from the Left, such as from Noam Chomsky who wrote about 'manufacturing consent,' and the great Jacques Ellul who wrote about democracy and propaganda (Ellul was more of an anarchist). There are a few vocal voices on this side of politics interested in the truth these days though most are too busy sipping chardonnay, enjoying university tenure, and getting their kids through the best schools. If this minority on the Left realized that there were a few on the Right who shared most of their world view, then we would be witnessing a remarkable coalition of mutual interests, though they are too busy hating each other these days, and arguing over battles no one remembers or cares about.

It is, however, indicative of the times to blame others for fake news, for curated content, and for media manipulation as if there is a chasm between us and the political system or economic system in our society. *'It's the media barons to blame, the oligarchs, the special interests,'* claim many, arguing that our society has been ruined by these corporate interests who are pursuing profit at all costs. The last few years has seen many variants of this argument, from the so-called *'puppet masters'* of the World Economic Forum to Bill Gates, George Soros, and Hilary Clinton. If an oligarch's political disposition deviates one degree from our politics, then he or she is the Antichrist, but if they reflect and embody our collective hatred, then they are doing the will of God.

Anyone who runs a business knows that you have to give people what they want and even if there is a subtle manipulative process underway in marketing, it is not as simple as opening a glass jar and pouring in some jam. We, as consumers, still have some degree of autonomy, some degree of choice, and some degree of discernment when it comes to buying, selling, and engaging in the commercial world. In a democracy, we voluntarily concede our power to those whom we elect and whom we believe will ostensibly act on our behalf, but at the same time, we refuse to challenge the party system in Australia, or America, and so we settle for whichever monkey offers the best bunch of bananas come election time. The President of America will be a Republican or Democrat and that is as diverse as this robust democracy will allow.

Many people hated Donald Trump and many hated Barack Obama. Many despise sleepy Joe Biden. I have not met any of them. I don't know what I would say if I met them. I am quite sure how they are among their friends and family is different to their media image. They are not individuals in the sense that Bob Mitchell is, the guy down at the auto store, or Elsbeth McEvoy, the lady at the post office. They are carefully created, crafted, curated beings, marketable commodities. They are not free, nor are they without their minders, and the people who pull the strings from behind. They have powerful financial backers, each with their lists of demands and interests, and despite all their rhetoric, it is quite unlikely that at any point during their tenure, their real personal opinions, thoughts, and ideas were able to overcome the special interests that put them there. That is democracy, or Western democracy, certainly the democracy of America. The President reflects the special interests that shape the character, the future, and the directions of America.

But we need to go deeper than a critique of the personalities of those who inhabit the Office of the President of the United States, and whoever controls their agenda. The people of America, despite realizing the fundamental flaws of the system, still regularly vote these guys in, even though the abolition of the system is the best way forward. Everyone knows the system is broken and corrupt and those who still believe in it are rearranging the deckchairs on the Titanic. But at the end of the day, you elected Trump, and Biden, and Obama, and those guys reflect the ordinary American voter. The same is true for other democracies. If the oligarchs are fake and Biden is fake and Trump is fake, then we are also fake because our leaders reflect a fake constituency. You get what you pay for. It is like the joke about the Catholic Church where little Billy observes his dad putting money into the plate and then hears his father complain about how awful the homily was. Little Billy chirps up and boldly says, *'well Dad, what do you expect for five bucks a week.'*

The point is that if the population was full of decent folk, hardworking folk, selfless folk, then the politicians would reflect the character of the population, but that isn't the case. We all bear some personal responsibility for the state of our society today. We cannot keep playing the blame game and blaming the oligarchs, or the media, or the Left or the Right. We need to take responsibility for our lives, and we need to accept that yes, we are part of the problem.

Fakeness is the language of today, insincerity is the currency and superficiality is the spirit of the age. Those fake smiles, those fake handshakes, those sparkling teeth, that false piety, that deceitful character is the staple of our world, and instead of building a forest of lush trees and green lawns, we have built a desert. A desert, as far as I know, is dry, it is parched, it is devoid of life.

It is into this desert of the modern world we walk, or we try to, and we try to navigate the terrain, and it is increasingly difficult, because everyone is telling us that someone else is to blame for all the problems in the world. It doesn't matter because our mouths are dry, our stomachs are empty, and our eyes are full of sand thrown by the wind. If we are completely innocent, and this is true, then it is not our world, we are trespassing, and we do not belong here.

The only exception to this is the fake climate change debate which spins a tale of secular guilt, that with every breath you take, you are killing the planet, so you need to pay for that air, pay for the privilege of being alive, and live in poverty and misery for the sake of the environment.

Why do I call the climate debate fake? Since 9/11, America and its allies have destroyed almost every nation in the Middle East to secure oil, gas reserves and mineral deposits to ensure that they control the lot – Syria, Libya, Afghanistan, Iraq – they already control Saudi Arabia – and now they are after Iran, to destroy the regime and install another puppet. They want the oil and the minerals to prevent their inevitable decline as a world power and do to the Middle East what the French and British did a century ago. They don't care about climate change, and the last thing they want to do is reign in the temperature of the planet, certainly if it means losing their strategic advantage. Washington supports the current genocide in Gaza. They need Israel there as an ally to support their agenda to control the whole region. If 2.3 million Palestinians have to die for cheap American oil, then so be it. Or do you think it is all about democracy? If you do, then I pity you, because if America will go to war against Iran to install democracy, tell me how long has America's long-standing friend, Saudi Arabia been a democratic regime?

As the bombs fall on Gaza, know that you elected the men who are doing it, and it doesn't matter who you elect, these national priorities in this democratic system will remain unchanged and yes, the suffering of others is the cost they will have to pay for your prosperity. It is called capitalism and imperialism for a reason. Many wanted to make America Great Again or if you didn't, many wanted to Keep America Great, and it is impossible to do this in this competitive system without someone paying the price. You have to pay more expensive prices for gas and for your truck, and they pay with their lives, their homes destroyed, and their nations laid waste.

It is all connected. Underneath this fake society is a darkness that few want to discuss, even among Christians because it upsets them during their Sunday singalong when they talk about how Jesus will answer all their prayers and give them what they want. It is in fact Joe Biden and his backers, God bless them, but they won't get any thanks whatsoever.

It is the failure of society to truly inspire us, which compels us to seek something better, and for those who truly seek, it is not the truth, for what is truth? It is not hope, for we dare not hope, but it is something that is truly lacking in our world today. This is authenticity. It is someone real, something real, something that rings true.

This search for authenticity is why I started Freedom Matters Today in 2021. I was sick of the lies of religion, sick of the lies of the state, and sick of the lies in society. Freedom mattered to me, I wanted to be free, and I wanted others to feel the freedom I had or at least sought to grasp more clearly. The lies of Covid Hysteria concern a terrain I have covered before in my first book, *Freedom from*

Fascism: A Christian Response to Mass Formation Psychosis (2022). There was anger in these words, a righteous anger, an anger that our institutions had failed us, that those in whom we trusted betrayed us, and that evil was upon us. I remain convinced that I was right. I made a lot of enemies at that time and a few friends, but it started something.

Before the pandemic, I was a serving priest in the Anglican Church of Australia. Before vaccine passports, martial law, lockdowns, and Covid Theology, I was ordained first as a deacon and then as a priest. At the time it was a great honor. I took my vocation seriously and served my parishes with distinction and diligence. As I was serving in a traditional diocese, (geographical area), I wore the black clerical shirts, cassocks, and other ceremonial garb during religious services. People knew me as I took the time to get to know them. I was known about the towns and people greeted me on the streets and welcomed me into their homes. I followed the rules, canons, and statutes of my church with dutiful allegiance to the best of my ability.

In hindsight, there were so many rules, so many regulations, so many traditions, all invented by men (women had no role in the past) who neither knew God, nor cared one bit for anyone outside the class structures of the established church, or the church of Old Money.

Before the Second World War, most churches in the

Anglican tradition had the pew rental system, which meant that wealthy families would rent a seat, and this meant only the rich went to church, as it was only the rich who could afford to attend. The poor, well, no one cared about them, and the church, least of all. They couldn't go to church, even if they wanted to.

The story of my eventual acceptance in the Anglican Church is a long and complicated one, and a story for another time, but despite its class pretensions and hypocrisies, and appalling history, it nominally held to a number of ideas about God and faith that resonated with me and so I was, to some degree, happy there.

I grew up with a simple faith, and before entering the Christian ministry strongly believed in freedom, for I saw in the life of Jesus a freedom that made perfect sense. I experienced forms of Christian worship that embraced this freedom, especially in Japan, when people put away their differences and came together with a simple faith, questions, doubt, and a genuine love for each other that transcended culture.

I approached seminary with this background, a love for freedom, a love for the fellowship of the Spirit, and a genuine belief that faith was intensely personal and involved a search for the authenticity in the life of Jesus which is our motivation for a life serving the Father of the Son. Much to my surprise, seminary was the opposite. It was rules, regulations, ritualism, and a cold, clinical legalism shrouded by class relations. What mattered to seminary in Australia was my postcode, and my class background.

As God would have it, the more seminaries I attended the more I encountered the way that Christians have sought to capture, control, and conquer God in liturgy, words, and organization. Faith was about obedience, Moses soon turned up and attended almost every class, and Billy Sunday was there too with his strict rules on alcohol and personal morality.

I realized that the Western understanding of God was that the less we think about him the better, and God help us if we try to follow him. All that mattered was our group, our sect, our club, and all we needed to know was who was to blame for all the problems in the church. If we said the right things, mouthed the right mantras and spoke to the right people, then our future was secure.

I discovered in Sydney that all that mattered was keeping the ship afloat – the role of the minister or priest was to keep the money flowing in, and the doors open. When I moved to the country, and served in the rural parishes, I could not accept the unacknowledged, unaccepted, and unbelievable history of violence towards the aboriginal people who used to live in the area. A deep, abiding racism was still present in these churches, a loathing of aboriginal people, and a kind of Christianity that one could only call a variant of *'white supremacy.'* The towns had moved on, and there was more ethnic diversity, but the churches were, overall, relics of an era that most Australians today wished never happened which continues to cast a dark shadow over everything we do. I don't believe that God cares much for our properties and church buildings and so I proposed we sell them off to provide compensation for the victims of child abuse in churches and church institutions. Anglicans love properties and buildings more than they love God, so they were not pleased.

In March of 2020, the nightmare began in Australia, of martial law, lockdowns, and vaccine corruption. Instead of resisting tyranny, the Anglican Church, both the evangelicals and the Catholics, supported martial law, and invented Covid Theology. For me, this was, and remains a betrayal not only of the good news of Jesus, but also it was the behavior of Judas, for the churches lined up to receive their cut, their share, and their thirty pieces of silver in the Job Keeper slush fund. For all their fine talk, rhetoric, and ideals, the evangelicals are just as corrupt, wretched, and spiritually bankrupt as the High Church, their fake rituals, and reimagined pseudo-English Catholicism.

Deep down in my heart, I knew this to be the case, for I had also been to the Holy Land of Evangelicalism in Australia, Moore College in Newtown, and it was nothing more than a stylish country club for rich kids and their devoted disciples. The diocese of Sydney, late from the Indian Mission, should be called the Dynasty of Sydney, for that is what it was.

Like the Puritans, John Wesley, George Whitfield, and many others, I'd had enough. I wanted freedom, freedom from church corruption and double standards, freedom from a religion where God played favorites, and freedom from political tyranny that was nothing more than a descent into fascism. I decided like Wesley that the world was my congregation, and that my vocation was outside the church, where Jesus would be, because he would certainly not be welcome in church. It was the inevitable acceptance of what was already in my heart, and had been for many years, a love for all people, and a belief that the good news of Jesus was not just for a tiny group of people who entered a building on Sunday morning.

Freedom Matters Today was born in 2021, at the height of Covid Hysteria. Thank God for Covid-19, not for the hideous suffering it wrought in society, but through it, I could see the world more clearly. It brought light into darkness. I understood, for the first time, how everything worked together, a glimpse into eternity, and all the misgivings, uncertainties, and doubts about organized religion were brought to the surface and exposed for what they are.

Collectively, we could more ably discern the pernicious agenda underway in the West, that of a dying power unable and unwilling to accept the logic of history that everything dies, everything comes to an end, and that everything has a time. We were witnessing the death-throes of a superpower in reluctant decline, content to bring down the entire world into a nightmare of war, imperialism, fascism, and death. This is the nation of America, the nation most Christians in the West see as the light on the hill, the beacon for the gospel, the source of all goodness. They could never be more wrong, they could never be more mistaken, and they could never be more perilously misguided.

By throwing all their support behind Washington and its priorities, Christianity is in serious danger of extinction and so that is why politics matters. Just look at the Middle East. American foreign policy since 9/11 effectively wiped-out Christian witness in that part of the world, Christian communities that have stood for centuries as minorities in an Islamic world. The decline of America is not the end of Western values, it is not the termination of Western civilization, it is not even the end of America, but it is simply a readjustment to the capitalist imperatives of our economy and society, and these dynamics are pushing other more competitive nations to the fore. This is what capitalism is – rapacious, and unforgiving. Without war, the future will be a quieter America, a slower Europe, a sleeping Japan, a revived Russia, a robust China, and a noisy India. America and Britain are at war with Russia, America runs Japan, and America wants war with Iran and China and is complicit in the genocide in Gaza.

For the first two years of Freedom Matters Today, my focus was on encouraging my readers and listeners not to go to church, but to follow Jesus instead. Churches are not safe places; they are not places where anyone is welcome. They are toxic institutions of abuse. This was deeply offensive to the men and women who derive their prosperity from the church, as I was seeking to remove their source of wealth. One of my goals is to abolish the charity status for religions that will end most of their problems and allow them to see God more clearly in a competitive market system, rather than covet their property and wealth like Smaug the Desolate coveted gold in Tolkein's Hobbit. Free from the charity prison, church pastors, priests, bishops, and ministers might have to pray to the God they pretend to believe in, at least on Sunday.

I was and remain concerned for the many millions of people hurt, abused, bullied, cast out and persecuted by religion but for whom Jesus came, bled, and died. Jesus came for those whom the church rejects, which is most people. Who will stand for them? Who will help them? As a priest, I had no favorites, I saw all people as the same, even in the nursing homes and hospitals, I administered care to all, and without exception. This was the wrong approach apparently, for the priest must only look after his people, not others, but I don't accept that. All in need are those for whom God came.

I have argued in my books and have firmly believed in the past that church attendance is not mandatory for Christians but following Jesus is, and that in following Jesus, we are living out the purpose, plan, and power of God in our lives.

In the middle of 2023, it occurred to me that if we are to follow Jesus, then we need to know who he is, we need to understand how he saw himself and how others saw him, and we need to ponder his identity. His identity was what got him killed, not the resurrection, and his identity is what we need to understand today. For me, my interest in Jesus is not simply because he is the founder of Christianity. Jesus lived an authentic life, and this authenticity is important because it resonates deeply with the needs of people today, to overcome the fake culture, the fake society, and the fake lives we are all living. We need something real; we need someone real, and for me, we need to know the real Jesus. If *'knowing Jesus'* is simply code for *'turning up on Sunday,'* then we will remain in ignorance. Most people who go to church do so out of ritual or fear, or obligation, have no idea who God is and certainly don't know much about the Jesus they sing about every Sunday.

Most of my books have been about setting up the proposition that following Jesus is at the heart of the life of a person who claims to be a Christian. *'Is Russia Our Enemy?'* and *'Is God on America's Side?'* are books that study various aspects of our lives in relation to this central proposition, that a Christian is a person who follows Jesus. The former book studied the spiritual dimension of our lives, the contest between our enemy, diabolos, and Jesus, in the wilderness. The latter examined the public aspects of our life, citizenship, speech, and living in community with others. *'Following Jesus when the church has lost its way,'* was a book looking at the various aspects of personal freedom that comes from knowing God and his Son Jesus. My other books, *'Freedom from Fascism,' 'The Lies, Legacies and Lessons of Covid Hysteria,'* and this one dealt with the intersection of faith and flag, of church and state, of faith and citizenship, and the various dimensions of the nightmare of Covid Hysteria.

My book *'What are the Pronouns of God?'* began my pivot away from Covid Hysteria towards the identity of Jesus. It was a difficult book to write because I want to write in such a way that anyone can understand what I am saying without any prior knowledge. Like *'Following Jesus when the Church has lost its way,'* this book is practical and pastoral.

This book is my seventh title in the Freedom Matters Today series in what I have come to call *'Phase 1.'* It is a series of on the record conversations about Covid Hysteria, God, Fascism, and the West, recorded in eleven interviews conducted during 2023. I used the transcription function on Microsoft Word to create the original file and then went back through the interviews to polish them and remove mistakes. They are, to the best of my ability, what I said and what was said during these interviews. I have included the date and the link for anyone wishing to hear the original. Please let me know if I have made any mistakes and I will correct them. They are not official transcripts, but I believe it is important for me to be on the record regarding many of these issues, and for me to nail my colors to the mast, instead of ducking for cover, putting my head in the sand, or jumping ship as so many Christians are doing these day.

This is the time for Christians to stand up and speak truth to power, both secular and religious. If this is not possible, and for most people, it is not, it is time to speak the truth about power, both secular and religious. This means in your family, amongst your friends, in your social circle, and in your community. Covid Hysteria, Gaza Genocide, American foreign policy, Covid Theology, are all issues that affect us all, and are not marginal or irrelevant to our faith in Jesus, or our walk with him.

Our world is fake, our society is fake, our churches are fake, and we need therefore, to refuse to see the world as it is presented to us and refuse to play by the rules of the world. We need to return to God, embrace the authenticity of the Son and follow Jesus wherever he leads us. Jesus came to set us free, and to experience real freedom.

We can, because we follow Jesus, experience freedom from fascism and tyranny, freedom from fear and despair, freedom from sin and death, freedom from guilt and shame, freedom from past and prejudice, and freedom from war and conflict. Freedom matters today because we all matter to God.

2

MAY 16, 2023

Interview with Neil Johnson, on the 20Twenty Vision Podcast, Christian Vision Media.

https://omny.fm/shows/20twenty/the-fight-for-freedom-is-only-just-beginning-rev-d

Topics: Freedom, Covid, Vaccine Passports, Covid Theology, Propaganda, Mass Formation Psychosis

TRANSCRIPT

Neil: Perhaps nothing has looked so much like a war on our freedoms than the crisis brought on by the COVID pandemic. Our freedoms were evaporating before our eyes.

But our special guest today says the fight for freedom is not over. In fact, it's only the beginning. He says after being told that the pandemic was our greatest challenge in a century, we're being urged to move on, forget about the past and return to a normal life. Well, in hindsight, it appears our political leaders were deliberately whipping up fear and accused of regularly lying about Covid. So, what lies ahead? What is mass formation psychosis? And what forms of control should we be concerned about? Well, our special guest today is the Rev. Dr. Michael Sutton. He's been a political economist, a professor, a priest, a pastor and now a publisher. He's the CEO of Freedom Matters today, looking at freedom from a Christian perspective. One of his books that was released last year, is called *Freedom from Fascism, A Christian Response to Mass Formation Psychosis*. Make a special welcome to the Rev. Dr. Michael Sutton. Welcome, Michael.

Michael: Thank you very much. Thank you very much Neil. Michael is fine. Thank you. It's a wonderful privilege to be here.

Neil: Michael, the thought of moving on, nothing to see here, all that went before in the Covid pandemic. What were your thoughts as you've been writing about the way our freedoms have been diminished?

Michael: Well, for me, for me, Neil, freedom is at the heart of what it means to be a Christian and I'm sure many of your listeners would agree with that. And Jesus said that if the Son shall make you free, you shall be free indeed. So, our freedom that comes from God is something that can never be taken away. But certainly, the privileges that we enjoy as citizens of this country were taken away from us for three years and we lived in fear, we lived under martial law, and we saw a degradation of political rights that we haven't seen in this country, probably for generations.

Neil: And what are your thoughts for Christians, and I guess this gets into the deep end early in our conversation, for the Christian thinking about tyranny, because undoubtedly there's some that you would have come across and there's some that I've spoken to that said, you know, well, we shouldn't be speaking out. We should just take it on the chin, turn the other cheek. What sort of imperative is there from the Christian perspective, to actually be someone who confronts tyranny, who speaks up when there's injustice? Any thoughts from you here?

Michael: I have a lot to say about that. We saw the rise of what I call Covid Theology. Covid Theology is the idea that we have to submit to the state. Whatever the government says, we need to obey. We have to acquiesce or abrogate our rights and so on. But the reality is it's a little bit more complicated than that. If that's true, then the Protestants then sinned against God by breaking away from Rome. It also means that America, the American colonies, they also sinned against God by breaking away from England, and it also means that Martin Luther King sinned because he engaged in civil disobedience to fight for African American rights in the 60s. So, it's not true. The challenge for Christians is to stand up for the truth and if that involves civil disobedience, or, in the case of the Protestant Restoration, it wasn't simply standing for the truth, was it? It was, you know, we see the religious wars. These were Christians who felt that they couldn't stand by and live under Roman tyranny in the 15th or 16th century and that drove Germany and all the Protestant Powers too, I guess to go to war against Rome. And we saw hundreds of years of conflict. So, were those Christians sinning against God? I think it's much more complicated than simply, you know that blanket statement, saying that we should submit to the government all the time.

Neil: Interesting, isn't it that while our aspiration might be harmonious living in community and peacefulness, history is littered with wars and bloodshed and around issues a little bit like this, that have to do with freedoms and so Christians to take a mature view as a Christian, you can't avoid being involved in the debate. And let me come, Michael, I know that there'll be listeners who are fascinated with some terminology that you use in the title of the book we're going to be talking about, *Freedom from Fascism, A Christian Response to Mass Formation, Psychosis*. Lots of people might be familiar with some of the words in your title, but Mass Formation Psychosis might be new for some of our listeners. What do you mean by Mass Formation Psychosis? If this is the thing that we're in some ways up against, that might be taking away some of our freedoms.

Michael: Well, the reality is, Neil, that we live in a representative democracy and for representative democracies, governments, and society need to be controlled by propaganda. Propaganda is an essential functioning of a representative democracy, and propaganda essentially is this kind of indoctrination, I suppose, for want of a better word and Mass Formation Psychosis is a very technical term that some social scientists have come up with more recently to describe what we all know is basically a synonym for propaganda, and propaganda is at the heart of marketing. It is at the heart of, you know, public relations. When you go and buy a product at the supermarket, the marketers are there to tell you this is the best thing that you should buy. You need this. In effect, they're engaging in propaganda. We live in an ultimately free society. authoritarian societies, they just rely on force. So, if you don't agree with what the government says, they'll shoot you or put you in prison, but in a democratic and representative democracy that we have here, propaganda is essential for the functioning of society. But what happens, of course, is the temptation to then use propaganda as a vehicle to, I guess, manipulate and to provoke prejudice and channel and weaponize the population for a particular end and we saw that with Covid Hysteria in the pandemic and it manifested itself in a couple of ways. I just wanted to draw your attention to it and I'm sure your readers are familiar. The idea of "dobbing in your neighbor," is an appalling example. We were told to report your neighbor who attended a peaceful protest. There's no such thing as indoctrination in the sense where people become robots, not even in Nazi Germany, or even in the days of the Nazi party, were people becoming robots. What indoctrination does is it manipulates prejudice, it channels, existing pre-existing feelings, and so on and so the tragedy of Covid Hysteria with the police brutality and with the lockdowns and the vaccine passports, is it took our prejudices and kind of exploited us and channeled us into I guess in becoming weapons for the state and many of us live in shame. Many Australians live in shame at what happened, what they did, what they didn't do, and I think we're in a sort of a time where we really need to think what we did, what Australia did and really come to terms with it, we can't move on unless we come to terms with what was said and done.

Neil: So, in a representative democracy that we have, we actually do need propaganda. But you're saying propaganda comes in a good sense and it comes in a bad sense. And if we're not controlled by propaganda, we might be controlled by the gun. But propaganda being at the heart of marketing and let me just put you on the spot here because we might be concerned about what Christians think about this. Do Christian engage in our own form of propaganda? Is evangelism like propaganda?

Michael: Absolutely.

Neil: So, there are good uses of it.

Michael: Yeah, it's just a word. Propaganda is just a way of promoting a particular point of view, really. Mass Formation Psychosis is the idea of the malicious, pernicious manipulation of people, I guess trying to turn people into a weapon. And we've seen that with Trump, we saw the weaponization of the ideology against Trump. It will be turned against him in maybe a year or so. And then with Covid Hysteria, it took the government about six months to weaponize the population and then with the war in Ukraine, it took them basically a week. So, they're getting better and better at weaponizing the population for a particular end, and we have to be aware of what we watch on TV, what we've been listening to. We have to be aware of what people are saying, why they're saying it. And also, we need to be aware of how we feel about certain issues because I guess one of the great things about marketing is that marketers are able to find out the things that we want. And so, if you want to buy a bed or want to buy a chair or a table and the social media is on, is perfect at this, I guess on giving you what you want and that's a very benign thing really. Most marketing is fairly benign, but unfortunately, government propaganda, the temptation is so great for governments to use it, and that's what they did with, that's what they did with the propaganda under Covid Hysteria.

Neil: And I guess that propaganda, when you talk about opponents or alternative ideas or the prejudices that might be underlying there, so the weaponizing does happen when the laws change because we've seen so much in recent years of laws changing from what we held as those even Christian founded law say around marriage, and now the trans issues that are so prevalent. You know, euthanasia, abortion, and so the laws change and it weaponizes one side to use against the traditionalists or the other side that is holding perhaps to a biblical view, is that the way weaponizing begins.

Michael: Not really, Neil. Laws are just ink on a page, ultimately, and we saw that with the martial law in Australia with the Biosecurity Act that all the laws that we held dear, freedom of expression and freedom of assembly and so on, the churches were closed down under the Bio Security Act, which is effectively martial law. And so what happened in Australia was the suspension of democracy and democratic rights and freedoms, and so what the government proved both in Australia but also abroad was that the laws mean nothing, that the government, the state, has the power to change laws at whim and they did, and really, it showed the fundamental weakness in representative democracy that it's not a system that is any better or worse than other systems, that it is just as frail. And I think the reason for that is that it's made up of men and women who, though made in the image of God, have fallen short of the glory of God and that brings me back to the wonder and amazing truth that Christ came into the world to set people free from sin and to bring them back into a relationship with God. And that can happen to anyone, and no one is beyond the reach and love of God, even those in government who so vehemently hate the gospel.

Neil: Our Talkback line is open. What do Christians think about what lies ahead for our freedoms in Australia? What is mass formation psychosis? We've been talking about what that is, what that means, and what forms of control we should really be concerned about. Well, our special guest is the Rev. Dr. Michael Sutton. He's the CEO of Freedom Matters Today in his book *Freedom from Fascism, a Christian response to Mass Formation Psychosis* makes some big claims and some important comments. Michael let's stay with your book title for a moment. And while we've talked about mass formation psychosis, the way we can all get swept along in that, that you use the word 'fascism' in your title. I wonder if you've got some clear definition of what that means, because some people like to use that word as a weapon against people who disagree with them as well. What are your thoughts on fascism?

Michael: No, absolutely, Neil. We see people calling each other fascists all the time. Essentially, fascism is the voluntary conceding of individual authority to another authority, and we see that in in democracies where people have, I guess, offloaded their personal responsibility on to someone else. But there are many different types of fascism. There is old fashioned fascism, and there's new fascism, but I think from my perspective there are two aspects to fascism that are important. One is the mixing of what I call faith and flag. And that's where Christians confuse the personal relationship, they have with God with I guess, a national understanding of Christianity and the second aspect of it is the belief which I believe is wrong, that the past was better, but the Bible teaches us that all have sinned and fallen short of the glory of God and the gospel of the good news of Jesus is available to all. Unfortunately, fascists believe that in the past everything was better. The glory days were great, but today is a mess, but the Bible doesn't present the world like that. The Bible clearly says we are all, we all stand before God, we all are sinners, we all need the love and mercy of God found in

Jesus Christ and to trust in him as a call is not only for us, but for our forebears. And if you read the scriptures, if you read the New Testament in particular, it's like reading something that was that's relevant for us today not something written 2000 years ago because it's a timeless message, and fascists and fascism are the ones who say no, no, no, no, we have an obligation to turn Australia into a Christian nation. We have an obligation to tell people that today it's much worse than it was. But no, one thing I keep coming back to in Freedom Matters Today is that God doesn't promise what he doesn't promise, and what he does promise is that all who turn to him in faith will live. And a lot of things that we really fight for and want to believe in, we cannot rely upon because he never promised them to us.

Neil: We're taking calls. Let's take a call. Scotty is in Albany in WA. Hi, Scotty. Welcome along.

Listener: Hi Neil. Thanks very much for that invite. Yeah, I would only direct people to the Reverend's comments regarding the mass formation psychosis. There's a group online that promote the videos on this on YouTube called the Academy of Ideas, which explains the concept that the Reverend is actually talking about currently.

Neil: OK. And are you familiar with the Academy of Ideas, Michael?

Michael: No, not really, I did follow Matthias Desmet, who was the one who came up with the term, Mass

Formation Psychosis, but I am more of a fan of Jacques Ellul, who is a famous Christian writer in the 1950s who wrote about propaganda and democracy. So, I just assumed, and I've taken the line that it's really all similar in a way, the early, not the early, the post war writers who wrote on authoritarianism and fascism under Hitler did a lot of work on propaganda as well, and it's sort of the same sort of tradition that there's the potential for power manipulation of people through state indoctrination, which is very common around the world.

Neil: Scotty, have you got something to add further to our conversation?

Listener: Yeah, I think the current problems that we have with government going the direction they're going with regards to Christian philosophies are opposing them. While they seem to be, I think they need to get back to the original federal constitutional Commonwealth Constitution in 1901, which they seem to be ignoring for quite a number of decades, I would say, that goes back to probably Federation. I would suggest that the problem is people are not taught this in schools any longer, which is where the Constitution comes from, a basic Christian faith in various fashions, from a long, long time ago and goes back to the date of Magna Carta, it goes back 1500 years. And I would suggest that you will have to actually go back to the original Constitution and actual faith to be able to correct the situation, people have to learn about it, which are the basic rules of society, which then combats this propaganda that the Reverend talks about.

Neil: It certainly takes us back to the good old days in some sense here. Michael, you were saying let's not dwell in the past. The word of the gospel is relevant for every age. But when we're learning to live in harmony, in a society going back to the Magna Carta and those things that have actually birthed freedoms, freedom as we might define it under our own Constitution, what are your thoughts here for Scotty?

Michael: I think there are two things. One is political freedom, of course, and the other one is what I focus on in Freedom Matters Today, is spiritual freedom. You can be a Christian and follow God completely in a land that is oppressive and hostile to Christianity. What we saw in for example in the Soviet Union, you weren't allowed to be a Christian at all. All churches were banned completely. All forms of religious expression were banned, and yet millions of Christians lived out their faith faithfully following Christ in their own way, and we saw that also in Japan too, under the days of the terrible Catholic persecution, from 1600 to the 1850s. The remarkable thing was that when the Orthodox and the Protestant missionaries turned up in Japan in the 1850s, there were Christians who were living there, who had retained their faith for 250 years, and so the power of God, the power of God to sustain faith is incredible. I guess with Scotty is that I want to say that whatever governments do and whatever governments say there is no power in the world stronger than the power of God and in whatever society we live, and we can never avail ourselves enough of the power of the Holy Spirit in transforming our lives.

Neil: Scotty in Albany. Thank you so much for your call. Let's squeeze in another call before news. Alex is in Melbourne. Hello, Alex. Welcome along.

Listener: Yes, I just referring to the Bible as well with Covid coming on the scene and the government taking the law in their own hands, that I'm thinking like Babylon rising, showing us how it could be. That's all I want to say, alright.

Neil: There are some illustrations, I guess, in referring to Babylon rising thoughts here from you, Michael for Alex.

Michael: I heard that the one of the Chinese interpretations of Revelation, and it resonated with me. It's not a linear understanding. I'm not sure if it's true, but it's their understanding, it sort of goes in a cycle that every generation is confronted with choices and there is always, I guess, a Babylon there. There is always the confrontation, there is always the persecution, I guess, persecuted people who follow Jesus Christ, who seek to live out their faith, following Christ each day, they're always confronted by persecution. What we saw in Covid Hysteria was that the many churches said no, we will do what the government says, and we won't be persecuted. But Jesus said that if you follow me, you will be persecuted. So, it's an inevitable thing, I think for me is to focus on Christ, to focus on Jesus rather than on the tyranny that we face, because at the end of the day, we stand because Jesus stood for us and because we could not stand. And he fought for us because we could not fight and so ultimately it comes back to Jesus Christ for me.

Neil: Alex, in Melbourne, thank you so much for your call. Let's see if we can squeeze in one more before news. Hannah is in Albany, WA. Hi, Hannah. Need to be quick. What are your thoughts?

Listener: Oh, it's really great to have this conversation in the Christian realm. Because it's been hard watching your brothers and sisters' kind of not been discerning as I've seen it as I've struggled to watch. I actually felt a bit homeless, so I felt like in the church to put a mask up, to praise God or not be able to go to church at all. And not be able to have that corporate prayer and fellowship. Quite a few of us have talked about feeling quite traumatized and what I wanted to add to the conversation was with this mass formation psychosis, obviously, there's a sort of a brainwashing or indoctrination, so it's hard to see that when you've been deceived, obviously. But I think the people who are thinking about maybe we got it wrong or maybe we should have responded a bit differently. I think sweeping it under the carpet and pretending it didn't happen and kind of easing back into people's lives, who like me, we've lost our jobs. My husband lost his job. We had to pull our kids out of private Christian School, lots of changes. I think it needs to be on the table and people needed to humble themselves and talk about it to kind of heal.

Neil: Before we move on though, Michael, let's come back to the call. We talked just before the news. Hannah called in from Albany in WA and she intimated that she'd even felt excluded, isolated even in her own church around the way that the Christians took a position on vaccine passports and on masks. I wonder if you've got something to add as a response for Hannah and the concerns that she was relaying.

Michael: Absolutely, yeah. Thanks, Neil, and Hannah raised a really great point. And what we saw in Covid Hysteria was mass apostasy within the Christian Church. The government was able to, I guess, buy pulpits for 500 bucks a week with their subsidies of churches who adopted vaccine passports. So, there was mass apostasy. And Christians who closed their churches, who denied people access to the Gospel proclamation, who said that the funny thing is that with Covid Hysteria, you could have someone with, you could have herpes, aids, hepatitis, the flu, and early onset Ebola, but as long as they had their vaccination certificate, they were allowed to enter the church building. And so, for the first time in Australian history, well, probably not actually, there were pew rentals in the Anglican church before the war but certainly, since the post war era is the only time Christians have been forbidden by the state to enter their church buildings, and so it was terrible.

And as I as I've said in one of my articles recently, is that those who opposed Covid Hysteria, the nurses and teachers and doctors and administrators, managers and pastors, priests and bureaucrats who were fired for not being vaccinated, they all need their employment restored, their reputations and their income returned, along with written and public apologies from the institutions responsible. And if Christians can't lead in this, then I do believe that God will judge this nation. It's not about, I guess, judging God. God doesn't judge sinners for being sinners. He judges the church for failing to live up to what he commands, which is to be faithful to Christ.

Neil: Michael, it started off with Covid and their response, it started off just as a health response. It was a responsible thing that the government thought that they were doing, and it grew into a fascist response from there. How much do you need to be aware when there is change, when there is a new propaganda campaign to be able to discern and identify what's actually starting here. How do you make that sort of discernment when you think that the government has your best interest at heart and its just a health response.

Michael: You know, the temptation for government is so great that power does corrupt. We see it in the church. We see it in society, we see it in government. The power that people can have over others, the excitement that gives them the thrill, the sense of their own self-importance. I guess if you remind yourself that everything in the world comes to nothing, it all turns to dust. The thing that remains is God and God's word, and that our relationship with God is as eternal one.

We need to, I guess hold on to things a little bit loosely and be reminded that things can change on a dime, and we saw that. But the other thing is that, that people forget is that fascism is a lot more common than Adolf Hitler. Fascism was in Spain. It was in Portugal, it was in Chile, and in almost every case, most people went along with it. They supported it because the fascists, I guess, gave them a sense of national purpose, gave them a sense of belonging, but our trust, our identity, is with Christ, and so we need to soak ourselves in the word of God. We need to read the scriptures. We need to pray, and we need to seek, particularly pray for discernment, to discern what governments do and what they're trying to do to us.

Neil: So, if leaders have, as you say, a thrill of having their own self-importance and then imposing their will on others, is a good, correct, and Christian response to remind leaders that they don't have unlimited power and that somehow or other freedoms need to be maintained?

Michael: Absolutely. We saw this in the civil rights movement in America. It could never happen in Australia under Covid because the church told us that you're not allowed to stand up for your freedom and you're not allowed to resist government. But in in America in the 50s and 60s, you saw thousands of protests against the unjust laws against African Americans, and these were mainly led by many Christians like Martin Luther King, and they knew they were breaking the law. They knew they could go to prison; they knew they'd be arrested, but they had to stand for the truth and had the churches stood up for the truth, had hundreds of churches refused to close, then now as we see the pandemic narrative unravelling and all the lies about the vaccines and the vaccinated, then the church would be in a much better position, but they're not. They're just another group that was bought off by the state and many, many people can never or will ever trust the church again.

Neil: Again, that's a challenge and we'll get on to that in a few moments. The trust that we might have in our church leaders to be able to discern these things. Let me just attach something here because when we talk about the fight for freedoms, you're saying this is not over. Now that we're on the other side of Covid, in fact, it's just the beginning. So that might infer that there are bigger threats that are coming. There are some other clouds looming on the horizon. And so, something there for Christian leaders to be discerning and aware of. What are your thoughts here for bigger threats on the way?

Michael: Well, I just want to say something very, very unconventional, and very radical and controversial. Russia is not my enemy, and China is not my enemy. And yet we're being told by our government that we're at war with Russia, and soon we'll be at war with China, our enemy is not flesh and blood. Paul reminds us that we struggle not against flesh and blood, but against principalities and powers. And yet the Scriptures remind us of that enemy, diabolos, or the devil, was defeated by Christ in the wilderness where Jesus fought for us because we could not fight for ourselves. And we walk in the Spirit. And the Spirit enables us to follow Christ through all situations.

But I guess the challenge is for Christians today is to be aware of what governments want and what government wants is war with Russia. We do not want to go to war with Russia because they have more nuclear weapons than anyone and what astounded me when the war began last year in Ukraine was that committed Christians were not only supporting war with Russia, but they were also supporting unconditional surrender from Russia. In my view, a bad peace is better than a good war. The people who suffer in war are always the innocent, always the women and the children and the old and the infirmed and a negotiated peace is the only way forward in Russia, this idea that we fight them to destroy Russia is just insanity. And for war with China, which the government is, you know, the Australian government signed a treaty, an agreement for a $400 billion program to get submarines, which apparently are to fight China. But we weren't even told about this agreement, and this is what this autocracy is all about, is that these important agreements are being signed and negotiated without people even knowing about it. There are more Christians in China than are here. There are more people who follow Jesus Christ today in China than there are people who live in Australia.

Neil: I think multiple times over when you have those estimated numbers, but more than 100 million Christian believers in China. Interestingly, you're making a really strong point here and just to dwell on this for a few moments because as the Christian believer we're also a citizen of a nation, we're also part of this democracy that we live in, we have an opportunity to vote for one side or another. We're tempted to take sides politically, but I can hear something in the things you're sharing here is that somehow or other, our priorities need some level of adjustment, and I sometimes frame this along the lines of the fact that we're not necessarily as Christians, issues activists, but we're more along the lines to be ministers of the Gospel. What you're saying here is the gospel matters more than all of the issues together. Any thoughts? And any clarification on that sort of focus?

Michael: Absolutely. We have centuries of Christendom leading up to the Great War, which was the most atrocious war in history, worse than any other war. And then we have World War Two, of course, the rise of fascism, which is the great evil, and whenever fascism arises, it should be destroyed. But the best the West could do was one day, a Christmas football match where everyone stopped fighting on the Western Front. They could only do it for one day and then they went back to killing each other. And so, what we saw with the Great War after 1000 years of Christendom was that they could only stop fighting for one day.

I'm always reminded when I think of someone I don't like. I'm sure your listeners have people they don't like. And I'm sure that your listeners would have people they don't like, people who irritate you at work or at home or relatives, I encourage them to think about that person and think, OK, I don't like this person, I dislike them, I maybe even hate this person. And listen to God and God says to us, He says to us, Michael, that person I sent my son Jesus to die for him or for her. That person is not beyond the love and mercy of God. And then God says 'You were like that once. And I died for you.' And Jesus said, 'love your enemies. Do good to those who persecute you,' and that is the call for a Christian, which means ultimately, when you think about it, we don't really have any enemies except the devil.

Neil: And has some adjustment of thinking required, because we're also caught up in oftentimes the emotion of the moment and the judgments that we might have around the issues politically, especially. You talk about the new enemy. If the fight for freedom is not over, it's just beginning. You're identifying the new enemy, and we've been talking about that terminology, the fascist, but you also characterize that enemy as an autocracy. I wonder if you've got some thoughts here on what an autocracy looks like, what that means, and how it needs to be resisted.

Michael: Well, we, we live in an autocracy Neil. I was reminded about this by the Coronation of Charlie or Charles III. And so, we have a constitutional monarchy here in Australia. We know our head of state is a foreign monarch and he is in a sense an autocrat, even though he exists as the head of state rather than the arbiter of rules and regulations. For the last three years we've had autocracy.

We've had governments ruling and what's interesting is that a number of the fascists, or fascists wannabees in state parliament in Australia, many of them have gone in Australia, or they have tempered their fascist tendencies which is a great blessing, but a number of the real fascists have left the scene, which again is another blessing. But autocracy, I guess is not something that others have is something that we are heading towards and it's not only just for politics, but also for Christians and Christians have a problem and that is that when we give up on God and we give up on the power of God to change lives, we become fascists. And I guess fascism is, if I can give you an example, the Christian fascist, would say *'What would Jesus do.'* That's a pretty popular thing. But a Christian would say, *'What did Jesus do?'* And what did Jesus do? He died for sin, he died for me; he rose from the dead. What would Jesus do? Well, let's ask him. But as far as we are concerned, what did Jesus do is the most important thing. Unfortunately for many Christians we love a state that is, we want a state to be a Christian state promoting Christian values but every time that happens is that it's always a disaster because when you put five Christians in a room together, there is some agreement but eventually we start arguing about something as you know.

Neil: Well, Christians, we become comfortable, and you could call even God an autocrat that we would say Jesus,

King of kings, Lord of Lords. Our submission to him is above our submission to those earthly autocrats. Any thoughts here as the way that you know you, you actually do submit to the autocratic rule of the King of Kings. And that takes precedence over the other autocrats that are simply ruling over nations. Any thoughts here?

Michael: Well, one of the things I have is said that Jesus doesn't vote because he's the king, which I do like. But at the same time, we do have to follow our conscience. And that was, after all, Martin Luther, when he resisted Rome, which again was challenging the authority of the time. And he said, *'I can't submit to government; I have to stand with my conscience.'* And Christians during the Covid pandemic were told, *'no, now your job is to sit down and shut up and do as you're told.'* Churches, and many churches told their parishioners you must be vaccinated. You have to carry the vaccine passport. This isn't Christianity. This is fascism. This is tyranny.

And unfortunately, Neil, what's happening here is that the government knows in Australia that they can buy the church for $500 a week, and they know that in the Covid Hysteria is what happened, it was that most churches shut their doors until they were told to reopen. So, when the next crisis comes, they know and expect the churches to do the same. What we need to do is repent. The churches need to repent of what they did in Covid. We need to go back to the gospel. We need to go back to the freedom that God brings. And because when the next crisis comes, and probably this will be war with China, the churches will be enlisted to support it. And it will be disaster.

Neil: How do we restore trust in church? Because clearly this is an element if there are those who no longer go to church because they don't trust the church anymore, how do you bring about a restoration of that trust, Michael?

Michael: I don't think it can be restored, Neil, I think that the reality is that churches are in freefall and many people are leaving the church, but we need to make a distinction between the church and Christianity. Jesus is Lord, and we encourage people to follow Christ. It's interesting when Jesus met Peter the first time in John's Gospel, Peter says, *'get away from me, just get away from me, Lord. I'm a sinful man,'* and Jesus doesn't say to him, *'Peter. Yes, you are, Peter. You're a wretched, wretched sinner and he's all the things you've done wrong.'* He said, *'No, Peter, I will make you fishers of men come and follow me.'* And at the end of Jesus' ministry with Peter on the beach having the BBQ, Peter asks, *'What about John? What about this fellow? What is going to happen to this man?'* Jesus said, *'don't worry, its none of your business but as for you, Peter. Follow me.'* For Christians, we are called to follow Christ. And we need to walk forward, and we need to use the brain God gave us and the Spirit he has given us as well to make those decisions, but it does involve going back to the fundamentals, which is that it is for freedom that Christ has set us free and the power of God to change lives is more powerful than any power of any despot.

Neil: Times short. Let's squeeze in one more call. Andrew is in Emerald in Queensland. Hi, Andrew. Welcome.

Listener: Yeah, hi. Thank you. I just wanted to pick up on Michael's comment a moment ago about the church being bought for $500 a week and I wanted to expand on that. I'm wondering whether maybe the problem actually is when you think about the amount of money that churches and particularly Catholics get to schooling, in this country from the government, the tax deductibility benefit pastors get whether the government actually just straight up owns the church and maybe moving forward, we need to look at somehow disconnecting ourselves financially from the government to be a little more independent.

Neil: Interesting point there, Andrew and it could go across education. It could go across healthcare and the hospitals; it could go across an awful lot of areas. So, Michael, your thoughts on the fact that we do actually utilize so much of the welfare dollar that maybe the government does have an ownership already of the church.

Michael: No, absolutely agree with your last caller. We

believe in Freedom Matters Today that churches are a service provider, not charity and there definitely needs to be overhaul of the way churches are run. In the past before the 19th century, churches were businesses. They ran successfully, particularly in the mediaeval age. They were very successful businesses and unfortunately the charity laws do hamper the ability of Christians to I guess, pursue the calling that God called us to. There's so many things Christians can do, I heard one example, for example, there were some Christian doctors in a church who wanted to start a clinic on site just to help the poor and they told you can't do it because it violates the charity rules and so there are these kinds of examples. And so, for me, what needs to happen is the charity laws for churches need to be changed so they are businesses rather than charities. But it's very controversial. No one will listen to me, Neil, on this one. And there's too much money involved. But I do believe in freedom. I have an economic background. And I did see the fact that competition is good and that what you do see is that too much government support does actually hamper rather than incentivize organizations, and that includes churches.

Neil: Well, thank you so much to Andrew in Emerald and the time has run out. Michael, I think you might have raised a whole lot more questions that people might be looking for some extra response to and there's some challenging things that you've said, even controversial things. Some listeners might want to explore a little more, and they might want to connect with you even directly, and we have run out of time. I was going to talk to you a little bit more about the good ministry that you do with Freedom Matters. Today. But I'm going to push the opportunity for listeners to connect to listeners with the website freedommatterstoday.com.

You can also connect with Michael through brownstone.org and you can also access monthly podcasts from Michael, and he's got four books that are out. The one we've been talking about today, *Freedom from Fascism, a Christian response to Mass Formation Psychosis*, know that you'd be able to order a copy when you're on that site. Freedommatterstoday.com. Michael, thank you so much for taking some time, Michael Sutton. He's the CEO of Freedom Matters Today. Michael, thanks for joining us on 20/20.

Michael: Thank you very much, Neil. It's been a great privilege. Thank you and God bless.

3

MAY 18, 2023

Interview with Hrvoje Moric, on the "Hrvoje Moric Show," TNT Radio.

https://tntradiolive.podbean.com/e/michael-j-sutton-on-the-hrvoje-moric-show-18-may-2023/

Topics: Covid Hysteria, Tyranny, Ukraine, the Holocaust, Propaganda.

TRANSCRIPT

Hrvoje: Joining us is Michael J. Sutton, who started Freedom Matters Today at the height of Covid hysteria, when churches were turning people away if they did not have Covid passports. They were excommunicating priests, ministers and pastors who are not vaccinated, a time of lockdowns and tyranny, human rights violations, suspension of democratic rights at time of fascism and mass formation psychosis, a time of misinformation and fake news, religious apostasy and abuse of power, Michael Sutton has a PhD from the University of Sydney, Master of Divinity, a Diploma of Bible and Ministry, and a First-Class Honors degree in economics.

He's the author of four books. *Freedom from Fascism, Is God on America's side? Is Russia Our Enemy?* And *Following Jesus from the church has lost its way*, and he's also author of the novel *The Third Tsunami*. You can get all the books through Amazon. The website is freedommatterstoday.com, and you can find his articles at brownstone.org. Welcome to TNT Radio, Michael.

Michael: Thank you very much. What a wonderful introduction. I am overwhelmed. Thank you.

Hrvoje: Thank you. I'm overwhelmed by your bio and your prolific writing and production. By the way, I mean you've got a lot going on books, podcasts, writing, where is the best place for people to find you, at freedommatterstoday.com?

Michael: Absolutely. Freedom Matters Today, and if you want to subscribe, they'll get a monthly newsletter where I update subscribers, with what's going on, and also all the books will be, at the moment available through Amazon, which I find is the best platform, the most effective platform to distribute publications.

Hrvoje: Yeah, unfortunately, I mean it is the most convenient place to get books through Jeff Bezos's monopoly. But you know, it is what it is. And it's funny, you know, the theme that I just randomly was coming across through my daily reading was tyranny. I was going through some of my old interviews and came across talks like that with Gregory Copley of the Strategic Studies Association, and it gels up exactly with what you've been writing about, you know, the theme, which is like, let me just quote, he says, *"what we're seeing globally is the age of democracy, ending democracy as we knew it is gone. And we're seeing reversion to autocratic forms of government. In the West, we're historically we're entering what is called tyranny."* And you know, he's talking about the EU, the US, Canada, and Australia. And let me just quote from your most recent article, which pretty much lines up with what Gregory Copley was saying. You're saying, *"that after being told that the pandemic was the greatest challenge in a century we're urged to, to move on, forget the past, nothing to see here."* And you say, *"these are the words tyrants use and that is why for me there is a moral imperative to confront tyranny even within our sacred halls of democracy."* And so just your sort of big picture take on where we are, you know where we have been the past couple of years where we are and where we're going because it seems like, you know, tyranny is descending upon the land.

Michael: Absolutely. I completely agree with what you're saying. And for me, when I started Freedom Matters Today, I guess the oppressiveness of martial law which we call euphemistically 'lockdowns,' it was martial law. It was imposition of martial law in Australia and around the world and the suspension of democratic rights and freedoms, the abuse of power in Melbourne, police were running around shooting people with rubber bullets in Sydney, the military were marching through Western suburbs, which are the working-class suburbs not amongst the rich suburbs, of course, telling people to obey curfews, there was such abuse of power, and the word that kept coming back to me as s a Christian, was, *'freedom,'* and the churches at the time were saying, look, freedom is something that comes from a Right Wing, fascist view in America, that's nothing to do with Christianity. Your job is to *'sit down and shut up and do as you're told.'* And I've heard that before, of course. But what surprised me was that freedom was under attack, and in a way that so many people didn't realize, and I think at the heart of it, it made me think about what democracy is, and it made me realize that we don't actually have a democracy, we have representative democracy where we elect representatives every few years to act on our behalf. But what I came to realize was the heart of democracy is in fact the seeds of fascism. And it's always there and in a sense, representative democracy does eventually decay as the idea, the preposterous idea that everyone is equal, where everyone has an opportunity to have a say is replaced by a smaller group of more powerful people. I mean I can't call the Prime Minister of Australia and have a chat with him, but if I'm head of a corporation, of course I can. So that tells me right away that representative democracy is not based on the idea of equality. And so what we saw with Covid Hysteria was the acceleration of this process, that was very convenient to a lot of very powerful people who saw this opportunity to, I guess, fast track the destruction of representative democracy to the point where it is largely a façade, it's just the appearance and what we saw in Covid Hysteria was the demonization of the new group of people which really astonished me because coming from, as you know, the West is ostensibly a place where we like to believe that we are becoming a better society we are recognizing the rights of various minorities, we've fought for freedom in African American communities or aboriginal Australians in Australia and so on, so that's the process of freedom. But the opposite happened in Australia and around the world. We demonized a group of people who refused to be vaccinated and this demonization was so severe that it teetered almost on the idea that these millions of people are to be ostracized and destroyed by our society, and most people went along with it. And that really astonished me was that so many people supported the demonization of the unvaccinated and needing the term, *"the unvaccinated,"* seriously come on, I mean, such a bizarre term, and for what I was saying with my last Brownstone article, I think obvious that this must be addressed. We as a society, we cannot just paper over it and move on, nothing to see here. We must see and I've come up with six things that must happen. If we don't see them happening, then I don't believe we really have a chance, and we must see restitution for those who've lost their jobs. We must see restoration of their reputations. We must see reimbursement of all the lost income that these people have lost since being fired for not being vaccinated, reinstatement in society. And there needs to be repentance of those who have perpetrated this evil, and there must be the hope of reconciliation, absolutely, because ultimately, we're all made in the image of God, and if we can't, we can't acknowledge that, then we really don't have any hope.

Hrvoje: I think it was important what you said repentance because we saw months back, in the Atlantic and the mainstream media, which is a representation of this system, call for amnesty, but they did not, you know, forget amnesty, we need repentance. Amnesty is, you know, forgive us but we're not sorry, you know. No, no, it's just like you said, they need to repent. They have to say, oh, we screwed up. You know, those people need to resign. Some of them need to, you know, go before judges, and actually suffer, some should be, I think jailed or fined, and that sort of stuff. So, they wanted to get this *'get out of jail free card'* and I'm like no, sorry you need to repent and whatever you did wrong, justice needs to be served. We have to jump to the headlines.

Hrvoje: But again, getting back to the discussion with Michael Sutton of freedommatterstoday.com. Check it out. You know this age of tyranny we find ourselves in and you mentioned fascism, you know, for me, like plutocracy is too light a term, you know, we're living in an oligarchy, but it's really fascist and we, I don't think we're using these terms lightly. This is technically what we are now living in. People are having their jobs ruined for thought crime. They're being cancelled, some are being arrested in America and other countries for thought crime, for doing nothing wrong and you know, for me, it's just like, you know, I had my PayPal banned by the government last year and stuff like this and for me it's just my point there I don't care about, you know, losing that financial opportunity. For me, it's just I'm still amazed that I'm living through this. Like I can't believe it, and I knew this was coming for 20 years. But it's just like, ah, you're in awe, like, wow, it's happening, you know any further thoughts on this along those lines?

Michael: Yeah, absolutely. We're at the center of the storm in a way. Like it's interesting when you read history and you read about terrible things happening in the past and you think oh, if that happened, today, things will be different then when it is happening you do exactly the same and it's interesting. I agree with you about oligarchy and what's happening in the world in terms of the, I guess the awful things, but what I think people forget is that there are many different types of fascism not only traditional fascism. There was, of course the Nazi movement. But then also there was Franco and Salazar in Spain and Portugal, and they had fascist regimes. And the interesting difference between those regimes and the Nazi Mussolini nightmare that we experienced in World War 2 was that the Franco regime and some other regimes were largely accepted by the West, and they continued for a very long time. And most people embraced it, even though there was terrible violence. If you look at the history of Spain, in particular, terrible violence, a lot of executions, lots of deaths. But on the whole, the West just turned a blind eye to what was going on. *"Oh. Well, you know, it's just the Spanish way. This is how things are."* But as soon as Franco died, then the king stepped in, and that was the end of that nightmare.

And so there was a lot of opposition.

But what astounded me when we talk about fascism, is that people say *'oh, we can't get anything like fascism because it's not like the days of Hitler.'* But that is, I guess, a superficial understanding of fascism, because there are many different types of fascism. And as we saw with Covid, many people benefited financially from Covid Hysteria and many people in the ruling class, many bureaucrats, politicians, church leaders, the church has made an absolute fortune in Australia. They're laughing all the way to the bank. The Covid Hysteria payments from government was the best thing that ever happened to them. Some of them got millions and millions of dollars of tax-free money in their coffers and at the same time so many millions of people suffered not only being unvaccinated but losing their jobs, losing their businesses. Hundreds of thousands of businesses around the world went bankrupt because of the lockdowns, and it was deliberate. It was conscious, it was deliberate and ultimately, they got away with it. And as you know, I was listening to your news broadcaster and the conversation we're having before about China and it my belief that this is all fine tuning us to prepare for war with China, a war that would be absolutely unimaginable. China will not, cannot, cannot, like Russia cannot really be defeated. They're just enormous countries, powerful countries.

But there's this bizarre belief that we can just go in, and we can take out China and we're being prepared, I guess, for that scenario, and more and more people are saying and believing things that even five years ago you would dismiss them as nutters *(Slang for crazy people – Editor)*. And when, for example, when the conflict began in Ukraine, some saying the conflict continued in Ukraine, in February, many American talk show hosts were talking about nuking Russia and assassinating Putin using nuclear weapons. This is crazy talk. Instead of shutting these interviewers down and just shutting them off, turning them off, they were allowed to spout this nonsense. Nuclear war will result in the death, or the complete decimation of the human race. The entire nuclear arsenal is on automatic pilot, and it will just continue for month after month after month and every single person on the planet will die. But what's astounded me in the last few months, the last year or so is that so many people in the ruling class believe that war with Russia and war with China would result in a triumph on one side or the other. And this is insanity. And perhaps this is the insanity that comes from the reality that the West is declining, every dog has its day, as we say, every empire collapses eventually. If you want to see. the future of America, go to a museum and look at what happened to all the empires of the past, and unfortunately what we see in Australia and America and in Europe is this refusal to accept reality that eventually what we have and what we love comes to an end. This is a microcosm of life in a way.

Hrvoje: There's so much there in what you just said and its great analysis, obviously, very dark analysis, but it kind of confirms my view, so I feel like I'm not crazy that I'm thinking on the right track. I am seeing things as, you're seeing them and I, would agree with you, it seems like they're preparing for war with Russia and China, Third World War. It seems like for some reason that you know it, it eludes us that these elites for some reason, by hook or by crook want it so much, its hard to fathom why they're a bit crazy. I think they just want to take over the world. I think they want to use the destruction that comes from the war to remake the world afterward. But just to go back to what you were saying about how so many people went along, we saw it pretty much everywhere during COVID-19 84, as I call it, I was in multiple countries, yeah, and you know it's the Stockholm Syndrome and every time in history, as you mentioned in the 30s in Spain and Germany, people largely seem to go along. One of the most instructive books for me that I read a long time ago is a historian was Milton Mayers, *'They thought they were free,'* and I think he was a German American Jew and he interviewed a dozen average Germans, You know, that's like subjects, (and he did not tell them that he was Jewish), teachers, bakers, business people to understand how it was that they went along, you know, with the Nazi regime, some of them just turned a blind eye. Some of them were just in it for the money to keep their job, their status. You know, I think many were not even, not Nazis, you know, passionate Nazis. And it's like we saw the same thing with Covid you just outlined it, the churches or people wanting to keep their jobs. I know a handful of people who lost their jobs because they refused to be injected. You know, they were willing to have that defiance. Do you have any thoughts as to why this is? It seems like it's a thing that's static in history, it doesn't change. It always happens when we go through tyranny where very few people resist.

Michael: But I think you're right. I think it's interesting because there's a lot of talk about propaganda and mass formation psychosis and so on. And I think what a lot of people misunderstand about propaganda and indoctrination is that we are not robots we don't, unless you're really a government, you know, agent or whatever or some organization really wants to completely weaponize you that it takes a great deal of intense psychological abuse to force someone to do what they don't want to do but, but basically propaganda, what it does it fine tunes our existing prejudice and exploits it for good or for ill. Marketing is important in this, we see with social media the way that you know you buy a phone and then the next day you get 30 ads for phones, so the AI is intuitively responding to your preferences, and that's sort of what propaganda is, but pernicious propaganda exploits the existing prejudice to the point where it can be weaponized. And a lot of prejudice is completely irrational. And it doesn't make any sense. I'm researching a book on fascism, the origins of fascism, and unfortunately, I had to read a book which I won't mention. But you probably know the name of it written by a lunatic in the 1920s in Germany and his book became very popular to the point where according to the preface written by Jewish journalist who was persecuted during the Holocaust. He said that it was given out as wedding presents to German couples, and I tried to find a quote from this book. And I found a copy of it somewhere in one of the libraries and what astounded me was I couldn't read the book. It was unreadable. It was a 300-page bile ridden written journey of hate and hatred towards Jewish people, hatred towards everyone and I couldn't read it. It was an unreadable book. It made absolutely no sense. It was just the author's tirade of hate. But the funny thing is, it was a popular book. At that time people read it and they loved it and I thought that was a bit of an insight into the irrationality of indoctrination. And that's why there's so much guilt in Germany because people, their prejudice that was existing there beforehand, was exploited by these people. It was weaponized. It was irrational. It didn't make any sense. But the result of it was genocide and the Holocaust. And we saw this with Covid Hysteria. People who dobbed in their neighbors: - they didn't like the neighbors. They can pretend that they were upstanding citizens, but if you love your neighbors, you supported your neighbors, you wouldn't betray them. It doesn't matter whatever incentive you were given. So, what happened in Covid Hysteria was that it revealed the true heart of so many people and as a Christian, I look at the heart of man and the heart of people, and its wicked and we need God's love and we need the presence of the Spirit, to enable us to love others. That's my perspective on things. But ultimately what Covid and Covid history did was that it exploited the existing prejudice of people, and it revealed the heart of humanity, which is a very dark thing, and there's so much shame going around today and there's this, that's why, there's a need at least for some kind of reconciliation, and governments won't address it because governments are institutions, but so many people feel terrible shame, and I know a lot of people in Australia who were vaccinated who supported the lockdowns, who are now being forced to challenge their presuppositions and realizing that they were wrong and they do feel deep shame. But there needs to be absolute restitution and repentance. There needs to be some kind of reconciliation, otherwise we are heading towards a dangerous time and there's nothing worse than unresolved guilt and shame in the minds of people. And there's nothing worse than that on the national scale. And it's the responsibility of governments to deal with that, to confront these problems head on. Like maybe in South Africa, after Mandela and there needs to be this, otherwise there's nothing worse than this simmering underbelly of self-loathing, which is ultimately what shame and guilt is, and opens us up to further abuse.

Hrvoje: Yeah, that's important and powerful what you just said, where in general in life and I've seen this, in the many countries that I've lived among, all people groups to some, some to a lesser extent. But it's easy to hate and criticize and dislike it's harder to love people especially you know. Actually, because most people are difficult and it's difficult to love difficult people. I have memories when I was young, a teenager and just some of the things that I said for no reason, insulting things to classmates and people, and I look back in shame and you know, but you can always repent as you mentioned that earlier and change ones ways and that's what we need to focus on because you know there are people stuck in this mode of hate and we need to start loving one another more and more and say, 'Sorry.' We're going to jump to our break again. Michael J. Sutton's website is freedommatterstoday.com. You can subscribe there to his newsletter podcasts. You can check out his books on Amazon. And he also writes for brownstone.org.

Hrvoje: It's our last segment with Michael J Sutton, who does great work at freedommatterstoday.com. You can check out his five books on Amazon, and he writes as well for Jeff Tucker's brownstone.org. Maybe to get back to Christianity, you mentioned churches shut some for financial reasons and you know, when I was living in Kazakhstan, the leaders, they were forced to shut by the government. It's a semi authoritarian regime in Kazakhstan. And I know the leaders of the church there. We met secretly in our homes, and they would say, yeah, *'we know that this has nothing to do with health at all. It's it has to do with a lot of what the Bible has talked about, prophecy and this sort of stuff,'* and you know, I often recall people like Dietrich Bonhoeffer who participated in the conspiracy to assassinate Adolf Hitler. He was in America he could have stayed safely in America. He decided to go back to Germany, and he ended up after the war had finished and they hanged him. The Nazis ended up hanging him even after the war ended and he was supposed to go to his fiancée, get married and happily live life ever after. But you know that's the way the cookie crumbles. And you know your further thoughts on the churches, Christianity if you have any thoughts on prophecy and whatnot.

Michael: It was interesting Hrvoje about the story of Zacchaeus, who is the tax collector whom Jesus meets and then then he confronts Jesus and he realizes the error of his ways and in that story he not only repents and is reconciled to God he gets, I guess he puts into practice what he believes and then he ends up giving most of his money away to everyone he's offended so in a sense he shows by his actions that he is sorry for what he did and he realizes that he needs to amend his ways and that's why there needs to be restitution, restoration reimbursement, reinstatement and repentance by the churches from all the thousands of ministers pastors and priests. Many were expelled, excommunicated, terrible stories, and there also needs to be a thorough investigation because the idea of priests and ministers standing up in pulpits, talking about vaccine ideology is illegal. In Australia, it's a violation of the charity laws; the role of churches is to teach religion, not to administer medical advice. Priests are not doctors. So, in effect, any minister or pastor or priest who was preaching from the pulpit the vaccine ideology is actually committing a crime and according to the church's own laws they need to be expelled themselves. But what you did see is that what I do believe is that Christians want to stand up for the truth regardless of the consequences. And you have throughout the ages seen Christians who do stand up for the truth. They stand up for their faith and the church is often there to persecute them and kill them. And the church is often the handmaiden of the government. And if you look at, you know, America would not be here, it would not be there, if the Church of England did not persecute the nonconformists and they left and went to start the colonies in America. And such terrible things have been done by the Christian Church against people who really didn't disagree with the authorities in any profound way, except over differences to do with the Mass. Millions of people have been killed over the years, and over their opinion on the Mass.

So, for me, Covid Hysteria was just another shocking example of how churches are a disgrace in the West, how they really just showed their love of power and money. And I believe that they will not do anything unless their power, or their money is threatened. And there's a lot of, you know, if you look at the life of Christ and you look at the things he talked about, he said you can't serve both God and money. And he said that as a warning because if you look at, for example, the coronation of King Charles, the money and the wealth, the opulence of the incredible wealth of the church, you look at Rome and you look at other churches and with Covid Hysteria, the churches, there was this bizarre coincidence, and I can't prove causation, of course. In lockdown in Australia, the churches all shut down and everyone was very quiet and then the government gave them all, a lot of money and millions of dollars passed into the hands of the church, and they were very quiet and didn't say a thing. And the government realized as well that we can do this again, when we have another crisis, all we have to do to silence Christians in Australia is to give them a lot more money this time and who knows what the next crisis will be. What I do find interesting is that there is no talk in the church in Australia about peace. Jesus said, *'blessed are the peacemakers,'* and Jesus is called the prince of peace and surely Christians should advocate for peace around the world. They should resist any effort to promote war with Russia and war with China, but instead they're on the side of *'let's go to war with China. Let's take out China.'* There are millions of Chinese Christians, there are more Christians in China than there are people in Australia.

And then it goes back to what you were saying, I think before, our conversation with the idea of China and conflict and it is with the time with Korea, with Vietnam, the three major conflicts we were involved in, we had been involved in the past, they were all family disputes. Even the war in Ukraine with Russia. And these family disputes are very difficult because they involve people who have very strong bonds and we really shouldn't have anything to do with this, these families disputes and what we have of course is with China and Taiwan is that China and Taiwan are to be reconciled. Reconciliation is much more important than I guess resistance in a way, I mean a bad peace is better than a good war. And I think that's where we are at the moment but for Christians, they need to go back to what it means to be a Christian and that is to follow Christ and what we say in Freedom Matters Today is don't go to church, follow Jesus instead. Follow Jesus instead, church going people get deeply upset and they say, *'that's what we are doing,'* but if they were, we wouldn't be in the mess we are today because what Christ said and how the church behaved is completely different. That's why there are so many people in the world who are interested in Jesus but they can't stand the church, because what they see is this gross hypocrisy and double standards, and so at Freedom Matters Today we encourage people to investigate the freedom that God brings, and there is the freedom that comes from God and cannot be taken away and the power of God is more powerful than the power of humanity. But we can make a difference Hrvoje in our own lives, and that's where we see our main focus, these big picture things are important, but we can have an impact on the lives of the people around us. We can show God's love. We can live as Christians. We can think, we can reason, we can discern, but we can make a difference. And Covid Hysteria and these other indoctrination programs tell us, *'No, you're not important. You're irrelevant. You have nothing to say. You have nothing to add.'*

But I strongly disagree. 12 people changed the world. The 12 apostles. They changed the world. People can change the world; people can change the world by changing the world around them and I think for me that's what it's about.

Hrvoje: We're getting some white pills here, people with some optimism. Fight the good fight. We are two minutes to midnight. Dr Sutton, do you know any final thoughts? The road ahead and any other ways that we can resist the tyranny fight for freedom. I think, you know, Covid was the shot across the bow. And we've got more stuff like that on the road, further on up the road as Bruce Springsteen used to sing. So, any, any other thoughts?

Michael: I think absolutely. And God is God, and he is big enough to handle our questions. If you look at the Psalms, David asks God lots of questions. We should ask questions. We should be critical. We should be critical thinkers. We should question everything. We should be very discerning about what we've read, what we see on the news, and we should take time to be with the people we love, people we care about, and focus on those important relationships and not get caught up in every tiny bit of the culture war. We also need to decide which battles we want to fight, and we need to pursue freedom and accept that freedom is from God and that cannot be taken away. For me, it's that freedom is all about following Jesus, which I strive to do each day. And that's what Freedom Matters Today is about, trying to encourage people to know God and knowing God, we can know ourselves. I guess equipping people to take responsibility for their decisions.

Hrvoje: Yeah. And I have what you mentioned, that's what I also practice. I try not to get caught up in the culture wars, I mean every day, people are posting these crazy videos. We know that stuff is going on as well as choosing we need to choose to be smart, strategic, choosing our battles. The website is freedommatterstoday.com. People can get your books on Amazon, five books, including a novel. And your writings as well on brownstone.org, your podcast is on the website as well. Thank you for being with us at TNT Dr Sutton.

Michael: Thank you very much. It's been a wonderful privilege. Michael is fine. But it's been a wonderful. Privilege.

Hrvoje: I can call you Miguel since I'm. Mexican. So, Miguel alright, join us hopefully, join us again in the future.

4

JUNE 9, 2023

Interview with Hrvoje Moric, on the Hrvoje Moric Show, on TNT Radio

June 9, https://tntradiolive.podbean.com/e/michael-sutton-on-the-hrvoje-moric-show-09-june-2023/

Topics: Covid Legacies, fascism, American politics, Covid Theology

TRANSCRIPT

Hrvoje: Back on the program is the Rev. Dr. Michael J. Sutton, who's been a political economist, professor, priest, pastor and now a publisher. He's the CEO of Freedom Matters Today, looking at freedom from a Christian perspective. Check out the website, the podcast that he's got, books as well and a monthly subscription freedommatterstoday.com. Welcome back to TNT Radio Michael.

Michael: Oh, thank you very much, Hrvoje, it's great to be here, how are you doing?

Hrvoje: I'm doing very well. It's warm, still hot here in Mexico. How are things out there in Down Under in Australia?

Michael: It's quite chilly, actually. It's coming into winter, and it's a little bit cool, so it's interesting we're on the opposite sides of the world, but we're looking at things that affect both of us, indeed, the whole world, really.

Hrvoje: Yeah, it's getting crazy. And by the way, when people talk winter in places like the Americas or Australia, I never take it seriously because, you know, I've lived on the tip of Siberia and Kazakhstan and Mongolia, where it's like -30, -40, -50, that's winter. Anything else is, you know, not really winter for me.

Michael: It is interesting talking to people who are from very cold climates and so on. And so, it's not really winter, but there's some cold, and it's not really summer. It's sort of in between really. When it's hot, it's hot and when it's cold it's not as cold as Russia or Japan or around the other parts of the world, but it has its own style and it's great to be here, yeah.

Hrvoje: Yeah, I was listening to some of your podcasts for Freedom Matters Today, and I very much enjoy them. They're relatively brief or concise, well put together, thoughts and the way you speak is very relaxing and makes one contemplative, and yeah, so I urge people to find Freedom Matters Today. And you know, how is that going? And, you know, what are your latest projects that you're working on?

Michael: Thank you very much, Hrvoje, So Freedom Matters Today is focused on looking at freedom from a Christian perspective, we have a program looking at freedom from fascism and tyranny, which is what has our focus has been the last year looking at fascism in Covid Hysteria, and then fear and despair that comes from that because the Covid pandemic, has engendered a kind of culture of fear that goes from one crisis to the next. So, I decided to focus on those two things.

And so, I wrote a few books. One was looking at *'Is Russia Our Enemy?'* looking at the nature of who is our enemy, who are our friends or what does it mean to be delivered this world from a Christian perspective and take Paul as a starting point that we do not wrestle against flesh and blood, but against principalities and powers. There is *'Is God on America's Side?'* looking at the role of, I guess, how the Bible views our citizenship, our place in the world, looking at things like free speech, how we relate to each other. And I tried to give a Christian understanding of these important topics and a number of people have said they never thought about it from that particular perspective. And it's also looking at things like Christian Nationalism and what I call Christian Fascism.

And then there's *'Following Jesus when the church has lost its way,'* which is trying to help people to find their own path after Covid Hysteria following Jesus, where the church closed their doors and introduced vaccine passports and took the money from the government and they invented Covid Theology to justify their decisions. And millions of people put faith and trust into an institution that ultimately abused them. And so, with *'Following Jesus when the church has lost its way,'* I'm trying to encourage people to step out in faith like the patriarchs, like the people in the Bible who went out and sought their own people, sought their own communities to build new communities and one thing that I've been reading recently is the remarkable story of the United States between the War of Independence and I suppose the Civil War, where there's this great movement towards faith. But it wasn't institutional faith. It was ordinary people with their Bibles going out into their lives trying to make sense of God and faith in a new world and building these remarkable communities in the sense like a kind of a democratic Christianity in a way. And that's really what I'm encouraging, in a sense today, with Freedom

Matters Today, to follow Jesus, don't do to church, follow Jesus instead, and walk like the people of faith in the past and our ancestors who have done the same as well. It's interesting that Australia's made up of migrants, aside from the indigenous people who lived here. But the others who came from the other side of the world to Australia, an incredible voyage and to contemplate those remarkable voyages, they must have been people with vision and expectation. And I think we need that vision again. We need to see the world afresh, we need to rethink our place in the world, our relationship with institutions and the Covid pandemic has already done that. It's shown us that the institutions we trusted were corrupt and they can't be trusted, and we need to rethink them. We need to rethink our place in the world. And so, Freedom Matters Today is trying to help people to think for themselves and make their own decisions. We don't believe in; I don't believe in telling people what to think. I'm encouraging people to make up their own minds, which is what freedom is all about.

Hrvoje: I think that was a good point you made about, you know, the people that emigrated migrated to Australia and anywhere else. It does take a grit, you know, a mental vision to step foot on that, especially as often people with little resources and in many cases of life-or-death situation. And I feel like, I've been doing that for a large part of my life going to unknown countries and looking back, it's like, yeah, I mean, I can feel myself different from people who don't do that, and I'm not saying you have to, it's simply a choice, it's not better or worse, but I feel like I'm tired, like I can't do it anymore because it really takes a lot. And then especially if you have a spouse, or children, it's even more, you know, and it's just like I'm going to stay stationary for a while, but you know for those people that like that sort of thing, I encourage them, especially since it seems like the window might be closing on the ability to travel around the world. And Michael, we're going to have to go to our headlines with James.

Hrvoje: We continue our conversation with Dr. Michael Sutton of freedommatterstoday.com, check out his podcast and he's got a couple of books he's just published. And you were telling me you've got this book *'Monkey and the Castle by the Sea,'* which is, as you describe it as a little bit like *The Hobbit*, runs into *Journey to the West*. I don't know. *Journey to the West.* We'll have to check that out. But you say that all of your stories are about men and monkeys trying to find freedom in a mad world, and I think that's what a lot of us are trying to do. That's what I'm trying to do. That's what a lot of people on TNT Radio are trying to do and a lot of people that I've met in the real world, you know, I was at, you know, Derrick Rose someone, who is relatively well known in the TNT alternative media space, him and John I'm forgetting his name, John Bush from Texas did the Greater Reset conference a couple months back and I attended it and a Mexican company called, *'We are not Zombies,'* produced a 30-minute documentary released, about the Greater Reset where I live and that's a perfect example of what you're talking about, trying to find freedom in a mad world where all these people converged from all, you know, different parts of the world at this event, for example. And there's many of these events going on, you know, and they were all trying to find freedom. They all came from diverse perspectives and religions and spiritual, you know, perspectives or non-spiritual. But that was one of the main themes. I just from my personal discussions, people are attempting to find freedom, some are buying land, forming communities, some are more itinerant. And so, you know, what can you tell us about, after having written these novels, these books and in your search, attempting to find freedom in this insane world we find ourselves in, or Mad Max. World, that's fitting for Australia.

Michael: Yeah. Well, it's interesting. I think reflecting on the three novels that are written, all the main characters in all of them in *Monkey and the Castle by the Sea* and *The Third Tsunami,* it's about a Japanese man called Masayoshi Kato whose family has a dark past and he has to come to terms with it, and also in *Curse of Crooked River*, it's an Australian historical novel and the main character there, is

Nathaniel Chambers. Both men and also Monkey as well, they are all men who have either fought in the war or recovering from war, and so they try to make sense of what does it mean to live after a hugely traumatic event? And so, they are on this journey and what they find, of course, is that you bring what you've experienced with you because that's part of your identity as a person. But how you deal with that is different. That plays out in your relationships, and I think that's really, for our time, we've been through these traumatic events and in some ways, we do have to seek freedom, and we do need to be free, but also, we need to come to terms with what's happened to us and what is happening to us. And I think part of the path of freedom is not only deciding to be free, but also navigating a world which is trying to oppress us and being aware of those mechanisms of those processes that that are so subtle and so manipulative and I, for example, we've been out of lockdown for about a year or so now, but it seems like an eternity, and even talking about it, people saying, *'well, that's the past. Let's forget about the past, let's move on,'* But you can't move on unless you've dealt with what's happened, otherwise, you know, it goes against what psychology teaches as well and all the teaching in terms of the Bible as well. You need to, before you can return to God, you need to come to yourself and realize you need to be set free from your sin and you need to encounter God and to encounter God, you need to search for him. And in order to search for him, we need to realize that you're in a place where you need to search for him. But and I think for all the novels that I've written, probably unconsciously, because I wrote them during Covid, some of them had been written before, but then I re-edited them during Covid, and it's this search for freedom, but also trying to come to terms with the past but not letting that traumatic events of the past shape who we are in a negative way. I guess sort of taking the past but tailoring it to our, our present and enabling us to be the best people we can be in, in today's world.

Hrvoje: Yeah, you say that there needs to be some sort of reckoning. I was just yesterday, I guess there are committees or things like that under way at least in the US. And I'm a big fan of Senator Josh Hawley. I think he's out in Missouri, and apparently, you know, he tweets a short clip with Lauren Alihan. He says she's a lefty lawyer who helped DC shut down churches during Covid. and she wants a promotion to the federal court, and he says no and if you watch that exchange, it's on his Twitter from yesterday, Josh Hawley. I mean, he really just, you know, lays it down, lays down the law with her and catches her and the hypocrisy because they were shutting down churches because of Covid. But at the same time, they were allowing all these other protests, these same people, and he's saying, you know she lost some case because it was unconstitutional. She was trying to do something unconstitutional and now she wants to be promoted to the Federal Court. And then you had Congressman Kelly Armstrong, I've never, actually heard of him, maybe, because he's from North Dakota. But he also came out and said the CDC used the pandemic to track American's location data. This included whether North Dakotans were going to church or taking their kids to a game, emergency or not, infringing on civil liberties is never acceptable, and so there seems to be some sort of reckoning there. I also follow what's going on in my other home of Croatia. A politician called Martin Miletich is doing the same thing there in Croatia now. But you know, I have to admit that Michael, things do look pretty bleak because despite this respite, uh, you know, we're seeing them prepare, make preparations now for this global WHO treaty that's going to enforce like digital passports and digital currency, in many countries are rolling out mandatory now biometrics for all citizens and foreigners in all countries and facial recognition and all this crazy stuff and you know there's that, and then I'm reading just today, a man was arrested for being basically for being a Christian outside some Pride gathering. And he was just holding a sign on the sidewalk in a public space and the police arrested him. And then, you know, Canadian schools, we talked about this yesterday. They are making Pride Celebration for students mandatory, so you can't even opt out. They are forcing the children to go through LGBT indoctrination and so and then, I mean, we can go on and on. Roger Waters. He gave 20 minutes talk yesterday online. They're coming after him. And one of my past guests, the German Government now is coming after him because he's been warning against fascism, but because he's been doing it so well the title of his book, I forget, here it is. It's called *'The rise of the New Normal Reich'* and it includes a face mask. So, he's warning against fascism, but they have completely flipped it. There's no way they can miss this. They're doing this intentionally. They're saying he's promoting Nazism and fascism when he's been doing just the opposite. I mean, just so your thoughts sort of on some of these things and, you know, the way the wind is blowing.

Michael: Well, fascism is here. Fascism is well and truly entrenched. We're in the decay of democracy. And when you look at the rise of fascism around the world, there's lots of differences, but they all have one thing in common. They came out of decaying democracy and there was Germany, Italy, Japan, Spain and Portugal, there were the elites, the ruling class, they didn't want anything to do with the democratic system and they overturned it and put in a dictator or a regime. And in every case fascism failed. And the most interesting case of fascism were the cases where they were allowed to continue, like Spain and Portugal, and they were allowed to continue until Franco died, and Spain and Portugal are no longer the great nations they once were, and that was because they had fascist regimes. So, if you want to destroy a country economically, in terms of the long term and completely derail it, then fascism is your ideology of choice because fascism ends up dead because it doesn't allow debate. It doesn't allow alternative points of view. It does not allow dissension. In authoritarian regimes, the prisons are actually the colleges for the future leaders. So, what they do is they put people they don't like in prison for 20 years and then 20 years later they let them out. And they run the country. And so that's how they do it. It's fascinating. In China, a number of government leaders actually spent a lot of time in prison and then they were released to be put in government posts, but in the West, what we have now is we're heading towards a place where there is only one point of view and you're not allowed to have an alternative point of view. If you decide to disagree with the government, you are a fascist, but they are the fascists. It is interesting in Australia. A lot of the fascists who ran the Covid Hysteria nightmare scenarios a lot of them have quit, in recent months, quietly leaving the stage and I don't know whether this is a deliberate attempt by the government to get rid of them. One of the tests, of course, will be to see whether or not the constitutional amendment coming up in October to enshrine an indigenous voice to

Parliament, whether that gets up or not, I suspect it won't. But the government is definitely running this campaign with the view that well, there's only one point of view with our point of view, and there's no choice. And so I think it would be very interesting to see what the Australian people decide in October because in a culture, a political culture where you're not allowed to have another point of view, it would be very interesting to see the people of Australia voting against it simply because they don't like being told what to do and how to think, and that's where we've got to now, with climate hysteria replacing Covid Hysteria. And whole other forms of hysteria. But fascism is definitely here, and it's interesting Hrvoje, what I do when I look at the news, I don't look at the mainstream news. I look at the extreme news from the extreme left and the extreme right. What I find is that they both agree on so much you have the libertarian saying that the West is fascist, a series of fascist states. And then you have the Marxist saying exactly the same thing. And I thought maybe you guys should get together, both sides of the spectrum and work out what you have in common, because both the Left Marxists and the Right libertarians agree that we have a fascist regime in America and in Europe and in Australia and so on but they disagree with the specifics but what I find interesting Hrvoje is that it's fascinating because we have such a terrible situation with all the things you've talked about is that people are coming together from all different walks of life, all different perspectives in a way that they've never done before because we are facing a series of terrible threats to our freedoms and to our life in Australia and in the world. And we're putting aside things that divide us and we're working together with the things that bring us together and this is scaring the hell out of the government because this hasn't happened in a long time. And if I was in the government, you're exactly right. Persecuting the people who are promoting this, I guess a movement of fighting fascism. That's exactly what's happening.

Hrvoje: Yeah, head on. My guest yesterday, Professor from Florida. Dr. Robert, who you know, views himself as a centrist. And even he was just, you know, mouthing off saying like, it's unbelievable now it's you can't even be a centrist. You either have to be like these extremist radicals, which is to be establishment today, is to be, in my opinion, a terrorist extremist, as you say, fascist, radical, and to be a normal freedom loving, right, they're painting us as the crazies, and you can't even be a centrist anymore. And he was making a great point yesterday, that there's no center now it's one or the other. And now we have to make our choices. There are people who are afraid, and they would just sort of go along to get along and keep their heads down, and for me, those people are the ones making peace with the devil and turning their heads, you know, away pretending like evil is not going on, no, you know it's gonna cost you. But we have to stand for what is right and be, you know, antiestablishment, because the establishment is just absolute, they've gone completely off the reservation they are openly tyrannical now. And Michael, we'll have to jump to our break. I encourage listeners to go to freedommatterstoday.com, check out his podcast and his books. He also contributes to brownstone.org.

Hrvoje: Just before we joined, I read that Trump was indicted and you know, I was reading the comment from Twitter, Trump announces that he's being indicted by the Biden DOJ, he must report to the Miami Federal Courthouse Tuesday. I never thought I'd live in a country that arrested the leading candidate for President. This is a dark day for the US. You know, I'm not as interested personally in Trump anymore. I think I'm going for RFK. Jr, not that I really care about voting or have high hopes and any political solution, but still, it's unprecedented again. It goes to what we're discussing. Your thoughts on this.

Michael: Yeah, absolutely. Hrvoje. It's fascinating. You mentioned Bobby Kennedy Jr. and he kind of represents when I read his book or parts of his book, and I've listened to some of his talks so he sort of represented a part of America, a tradition of America that was very attractive back in the 50s, and 60s. It's an optimistic vision of the future. America, in a kind of a world that America can make a positive difference. That whole period was. That's the image that I have. I'm a fan of John Kenneth Galbraith, who was an institutional economist. He also worked for the Kennedy administration. And when you read him, it's a similar kind of thinking so the world hasn't fallen apart yet. There's a sense that nations can make a positive difference in the world, and it's just interesting. He's like a relic. Bobby Kennedy Jr. is like a relic of that age, whereas today it's like a maelstrom of chaos, indicting Trump is something an authoritarian fascist regime would do. It's not something that a democracy does. It's a tragic day but we've seen this coming, but when Trump was elected in 2016, the loyalty test was you had to condemn Trump, you had to condemn him, you couldn't support him, you weren't allowed to support him. But then when Covid came along, it was the same thing with the loyalty tests, you had to be vaccinated if, you weren't vaccinated, you were an enemy of the state and we're seeing this with Ukraine war with tennis players being forced to denounce the war, and this is the new loyalty test. These are all signs of a paranoid society, beginning from a fascist regime emerging from what's left of democracy and people say, *'Oh, we have a democracy, one person, one vote,'* but I can't call the Prime Minister of Australia. But if I'm the head of a corporation, I can get, I can probably get lunch with the Prime Minister.

So, it's not one person, one vote, it's a society run by corporate interests. And in a way, it's like the economic takeover of the state that has been long time coming. And that's one of the things that distinguishes us from communist regimes where the state owns everything but in the capitalist regime, which is what we have, the economic interests are now literally controlling everything driving everything and the citizenry have been in full retreat and the tragedy of Covid was that the Old Left and the Old right not all of them, but most of them, and the churches just all fell. They all capitulated. Cecil Rhodes said that every man has his price, and in the church is you can buy pulpits for 500 bucks a week and that's what was happening. Churches were not only closing their doors to people they were introducing vaccine passports, which I never thought would ever happen, and they invented Covid Theology, which said that the church is not allowed to ever criticize the government because the government is right, I guess that we have to always obey. We must always submit. But then when you look at it, alright, if you look at Protestant history, it means that the Protestant Reformation was a sin because Luther rebelled against Rome. It also means that the American colonies sinned for rebelling against King George and this bizarre theology that they created, essentially is to justify their, you know, their complicity in this Covid Hysteria. And that's the tragedy, isn't it? And it's the people that we thought would be at the barricades who were the ones calling the police and giving the police our names and they were the ones who were betraying us. And so, what it means for me as a Christian, trying to make sense of how to be a Christian in this world, following Jesus, is that every generation is given the opportunity to make a choice whether they stand for the truth or not. One thing I've been realizing is that there's no such thing as a stable society because societies are made up of people and every generation as they grow up, they have to make their choices. They can't just rest on their laurels and say, *'Oh well, our parents made the right choices, or our grandparents made the right choices.'* No, it's up to us. It's up to our generation and our children's generation. And we must continue to stand for the truth and continue to fight for humanity because there's always this conflict in every generation and it's the sadness for me as a Christian that the churches betrayed their faith. They apostatized, closed their church doors and they persecuted the unvaccinated, they preached the vaccine ideology from the pulpit, the lockdown ideology. And now they're laughing all the way to the bank. And unfortunately, people remember because they remember betrayal and churches in Australia are in freefall, in absolute freefall. I would not hesitate to say within a generation, Western style Christianity will be dead, in Australia, in a generation because so many churches just continually close their Bible and do whatever the government tells them to do in return for money and for their tax exemptions, which enables them to run churches into the ground and they're not speaking to power they're undermining the congregations and not even protecting their congregations. And so that's why I started Freedom Matters Today because I believe in freedom. I believe freedom is a gift from God, and I believe that God is the God of freedom. We cannot have our freedoms taken away from us because they come from God. But we do live in this world, and we need to navigate what it means to be a man or a woman, a mother or father, brother or sister, a citizen. And these are the choices we need to make. We need to make these choices we need to make these decisions. If we don't, then society will fall, and societies are not kept up by tradition, they're not sustained by tradition. They are sustained by each generation that comes through and that's why we need to stand together. We need to put aside our differences and work together for peace and for freedom.

Hrvoje: Yeah, just the last weekend I was in Texas at the Ron Paul Institute Conference and got to meet the great old Dr. Paul and I just noticed that next to the hotel was Joel Osteen's Church. I, you know, whatever my personal view is that he's a false prosperity teachers. I found that amusing, an example of church that failed. But you know, I totally agree with you. So many churches. I think your projection I think will be true and many other countries beyond, you know, just Australia. In terms of their decline, I think people in general are just having this attitude more and more than they'll just do whatever the government tells them to do.

And you can see this story during the pandemic, for example in my community here in Mexico, in one of our homeowner meetings, out of the 50 people that met in the evening, every single one of my neighbors is wearing a face mask. I was the only one and I'm not wearing a face mask. And that just shows you where we're at statistically. And I always tell people you know. People don't read. You have to read as you mentioned, we have to know the stories of the Dietrich Bonhoeffer's and the Martin Luther King and we have to have that ingrained, we have to understand the politics, how the world really works. You mentioned RFK earlier. I mean, he came out yesterday saying I'm not going to touch the Second Amendment guns. He was down at the border, you know, talking how we need to close the border. You know, Trump is now emulating RFK talking points about vaccines and autism, and I think RFK seen a lot. I feel like he's like in human terms 2 or 300 years old. He really understands. He's been through a lot in his family and so and he's trying to pull people together and he talks about hindsight. Bobby Kennedy was trying to work with the black people white people to bring people together and just one point of the churches, you know, my church didn't fail. They flirted. You know, it was like one Sunday or two. They kind of really urged me to wear a mask. But besides that, you know, I think the point here is not to throw the baby out with the bath water, there are people just stopping, going to church, stopping believing Christianity, what I think this was foretold that this would happen. There'd be a filtering. There would be a separating of the chaff from the wheat, true believers and those that aren't, so some people, I encourage people not to, you know, step away from faith. And then where do we go to find your work?

Michael: Well, Freedom Matters Today, check out the books I have just written the three novels as well as the books on faith and life. And your thoughts and reflections as well, I want to hear from people. I have a podcast as well. We encourage people to follow Jesus and the path calling that he's called them to. Yeah. So, thank you very much for that.

Hrvoje: Alright, we're out of time. Stay warm out there in Australia.

5

11 AUGUST 2023

Interview with Hrvoje Moric, on the "Hrvoje Moric Show," on TNT Radio

https://tntradiolive.podbean.com/e/michael-sutton-on-the-hrvoje-moric-show-11-august-2023/

Topics: Russia, Ukraine, Sanctions, Faith.

TRANSCRIPT

Hrvoje: We have returning to us the Rev. Dr. Michael J. Sutton, this time coming to us not from Australia, but from Russia? Interesting…Returning to the rebel broadcast is the Rev. Dr. Michael J Sutton, who has been a political economist, professor, priest, and pastor, and now a publisher, CEO of freedommatterstoday.com looking at freedom from a Christian perspective, he's got a number of books and articles which have been published. Welcome back to the program, Mike.

Michael: Thank you very much. Great to be with you.

Hrvoje: And you're joining us now, is it a secret location or from where?

Michael: Joining from Russia. Yeah. Joining you from Russia this morning, a beautiful, sunny day here in the Ural Mountains.

Hrvoje: That is fascinating, and I went to Russia some six years ago and had a wonderful time. The people were great, the infrastructure was good. And so, I had a wonderful time. And you know what can you tell us about, you know, give us a dispatch from being in enemy territory?

Michael: Well, it's a remarkable place. It's my first visit here and I'm amazed by people, places, and hospitality of the locals. It's like a hidden civilization. As I've told many people that we've kind of been denied access to, not only during this recent time, but during the Cold War in many ways. And it's strange, it's strange with several places this morning I went online to see what I could access around the world. I went on to James Oliver's cooking website. That's OK in the UK, but I couldn't get through to Yotam Ottolenghi's website that's banned. BBC is banned, but

CNN is completely accessible, so it's very random. If you go to the supermarkets and I went to an incredible one the other day I have never been to supermarket like that in my life, not even in America, it was overflowing with food, there was wine from Australia, caviar cheese and fish. All the products that you normally would expect were there, the companies that have left, there has been a vacuum that they left and that has been fueled by entrepreneurs and other locals. Some of these are now filling the gap in the market. A lot of companies have actually stayed. In fact, most companies *'Stand with Russia'* and they don't *'Stand with Ukraine.'* And many others are afraid of the government's repercussions. What they do is rebrand their products as made in Sweden, or made in Italy, or wherever, where in fact it's made in Russia. And so, its quite an interesting situation where it's not that Russia has cut itself off from the West but that America, and England in particular, have cut itself off from Russia and to give you a little example of this. I went to Sima Land which is an incredible place. I've never been to a corporation like this, we were given a guided tour through this place. It's like a wholesale, but they do, they do the production design and stuff and make a lot of these products. And we went into one of their many rooms. They have these enormous rooms where they do all their research and this room had hundreds of computer screens, hundreds. It was like a government building and these computers were looking all over the world and in the corner there, there was CNN playing live from America. We have this impression of Russia, in a sense, sort of cut off from the world, but it isn't cut off from the world. The West has extended this Covid Hysteria nonsense into this conflict with Russia, and so it's the Russian people as you know, they're beautiful people. It's a lovely place and great to be here, and I'm amazed that we can actually, we can actually communicate via zoom. Zoom is operating, Gmail is operating, Google is operating. So, the *'Stand with Ukraine'* movement is actually more of a political propaganda tool of America rather than any corporate reality.

Hrvoje: You know what doesn't operate my Dutch email service start mail, which is blocked in Russia and Kazakhstan. But I would add if you said most companies *'Stand with the Dollar.'* You know, they want to continue making money, but it's interesting, as you say, how some BBC is blocked and stuff like that in the East and in the West it's vice versa. The East blocks the West, and the West blocks the East. And I try to read Iranian Press TV, The Syrian National Press Agency, the Russian New Eastern Outlook. Those are blocked in the US unless you use a VPN, and actually even my VPN sometimes blocks some of those websites strangely, and so I have to turn it off my VPN, and so that's really annoying. You know there's a lot going on, but given that you're in Russia, you're getting the feeling talking to people, meeting people. You get this vibe which you can't get if you're not there in in Russia, you know it's very important. Boots on the ground. And so, you know what else is going on? What else can we dig into? What's interesting for you regarding what's going on?

Michael: Now one of the things that is coming through to me is the sanctions we have in the West, is that we talk about freedom, we talk about democracy, and we know during Covid Hysteria that already a lot of those beliefs and attitudes were done away with. We saw tyranny, we saw martial law, we saw the suspension of democratic rights and freedoms. People weren't allowed to protest, people weren't allowed to exempt themselves from vaccines, it was terrible suffering for three years, and then suddenly the West invented this notion of 'Standing with Ukraine.'

With Ukraine we believe in democracy and freedom, and it might have worked well in the 60s when people were kind of in the middle of the Cold War, but I get the feeling that a lot of people these days are waking up to the lies of Washington and the lies of Canberra. And the reality is that we are finding around the world that there are many people who do hold onto the same values we hold onto who do believe in freedom, but they are from the most unlikely places. I was reflecting on the, you know, the soldiers that were going off to fight in Ukraine. Some of them are doing it for money, some of them are doing it because they believe in freedom and democracy or whatever. But the reality is, that we in the West face this relentless, persistent, comprehensive assault on our civil liberties, as you know, on our freedoms, our beliefs, our faith and our very existence, and we have done so for years now, and these soldiers are going off and they're going to fight for what they believe is freedom but when they come home, if they're not blown to bits or dismembered, you'll be in prison, or cancelled if you say anything like, for example, only women can get pregnant, there are only men and women, having sex with animals is wrong. And so, what you have is this turning of the tide.

I was talking with this orthodox priest in Russia, and I asked him what the challenges are facing faith today and he said something that may not have resonated much with him, but it resonated a lot with me, he said. 'We don't have anything to fear from government anymore.' And I thought, wow, the tables have turned, haven't they? They've just turned almost 360 and the reality is, is that we have a lot in the West to fear from the government. People of faith, people who hold traditional values, have a lot to fear because those values are being overturned, challenged by the courts, challenged by the media and the *'Me-Too'* movement, the cancel culture also resonates with me too because in Russia under Stalin this was the same thing. People could be put away in prison, they could be executed, they could be imprisoned simply on the basis of an accusation. And that's what the *'Me-Too'* movement is today. These people can make an allegation and get someone, and it's believed, it's accepted as truth. But in the West, we are seeing a counter revolution in the courts. We saw, you know, with the American actor, some allegations were overturned. So, we are seeing a counter movement, but at the same time the shadow of Stalin is not over Russia but in the West. And for me, this is an appalling story. You had in Russia, you had 1.6 million people off to the Gulags, many more were killed. Their lives were destroyed simply because people didn't like them. They were just jealous of them and so they made these allegations and that's what we're seeing in the West as well. We've seen then in a sense, the darkness covering where once was the land of freedom, whereas in Russia, where they have had, they had Stalin, and they had a Lenin. Stalin was, of course, the worst of all persecutors, but in Russia the sun is shining.

Hrvoje: All right, that's at least we're seeing light come into the clouds somewhere, and we're going to go real quick to our headlines…We are talking to Dr. Michael J Sutton of freedommatterstoday.com and you produce a monthly podcast, and I think you put one out couple days ago and actually listened to it today, and I very much enjoyed it. And if we have time, maybe we can discuss that. But you know, you brought back a memory I had when I when I was in Russia, I visited Kazan, the capital of Tatarstan. And they took us to a church in Orthodox Church. And they told us that the ground was filled with remains of Russians from the Soviet regime. Well, first they told us, you know, it's a relatively small church and they told us that in Orthodox churches, you don't have pews or anywhere to sit everyone. I guess they stand and then they filled the physical space of the church with the, I guess, dissidents standing packed like sardines in a can and you know just one next to each other filled the entire space and they would be taken up to the roof and then thrown and killed down. And so, you know that that sort of stuff is what went on in the Soviet Union. And when I was in Kazakhstan, the former capital we attended church there and they told us that they had a small museum in the in the big headquarters church in the city and they told us that you know, throughout the 20th century, they built a church like in the 1920s, government would come and smash it. They rebuild it, then it would be appropriated. And that at some point in the Soviet Union, they just would come to take all the men, you know, 30-40 men and young men and they would disappear, they never came back and so that's what life was like under the Soviet Union. Do you feel that today Russia is some sort of safe haven from the globalists? And then, you know, also that the Russian Government did implement Covid technocracy. And so how do you sort of see Russia, whether it's a safe haven or whether there is this danger of the totalitarianism, this new form of totalitarianism, coming even into Russia.

Michael: One thing I saw was interesting though, was Russians have a lot of museums and memorials for things, and they do have a great sense of remembrance and the past, and so they're not that they're unaware of their past, they're aware of their history in many ways, unlike many of us in the West, where we kind of have to invent our history. In Australia, they're reinventing our history or prehistory and making it up as they go along. But in Russia, there's a very great sense of identity, forged in the pain of the past, and one of the particular events that really, I guess, is the pivot that is really critical for Russia is what they call the Great Patriotic War against the Nazis, and this was a horrific war. This was during when Stalin was the leader of Russia, of course. Over 30 million Russians were killed during the war, with Germany and Germay's allies and not a family wasn't affected and so it is incredible to have that experience as a nation. And so, they're very much attuned to what fascism is. They know what it looks like because 30 million of their countrymen and women died fighting the Nazis and so when you have a situation in Ukraine where there are, you know, there are a lot of Ukrainians that are neo-fascists, white supremacists, the Azov Battalion, and others in there, and there's a celebration of men who were complicit in the genocide of Jews, and they're very aware of the conflict that we're fighting today, and the key conflict is not really, it's not an ideology or a way of thinking. It really is the return of fascism.

There are many types of fascism. There is the, you know, the return of the real fascists, neo-Nazi, but they're not in America running around, they are in the Ukraine fighting Russia and there is this denial of their existence, which is astounding, and this is, you know, this is passively accepted by the Americans, but they say, *'This is not the full picture, the big picture. We need to look at the bigger picture,'* but with what I see with Russia is that they are fighting for what they believe is their homeland and in Ukraine, and I think this is what the West doesn't understand. They believe this is Russian territory and it's not against the Ukrainian people, but against what they see as fascism and American imperialism.

And there's some interesting things that even Wikipedia, they say in a story recently that Wikipedia is written by the CIA. It is interesting that even Wikipedia notes the largest population of Ukrainians in the world outside of Ukraine is in Russia, so they must like it there and after the war the conflict accelerated, in 2022. It's been going on since 2014. The West has done its best to cover up the Donbass conflict. I've seen a lot of footage of that while I've been here. I've seen and spoken with people who've experienced that, and its horrific death toll and the psychological suffering is catastrophic but like a lot of things in the West, we were just never told anything about it. They just deleted it in favor of the latest streaming service. But what's interesting is that the when the war began, though, not when the war began, in 2022, in February when the conflict exacerbated, more Ukrainians fled to Russia than to the West. And so, that is interesting.

What I find is that I believe that identity and history are very important for people and there's nothing wrong with your history and there's nothing wrong with identifying with where you come from and celebrating the values and traditions that you were brought up with and that are important to you. And that's what a democracy used to be. It used to be that we are all part of this experiment or all part of this society. But what we find in Australia and in America and around the West is that it's like treading on eggshells because you don't know what the belief system will be and if you say something, you are cancelled, and people's lives are destroyed. You have to apologize constantly in the West for being a white man. You have to apologize for your white privilege. And this is just astounding. And the rest of the world, including Russia and China and the Middle East, they look on the West with, I don't know whether it's hatred or just amusement or surprised thinking, *'what the hell are you guys doing? What are you doing? You're destroying your entire culture. For what? What's the end goal?'* And I believe the end goal is like kind of some kind of fascist state where the government basically controls us and manipulates successfully, they did with Covid Hysteria, but with Covid Hysteria, they needed an enemy and that was the unvaccinated. And the current situation was that Covid Hysteria couldn't be run forever. They needed something else and so they've turned on Russia. And then when this situation is over though, they will move on to somebody else probably China. But only an imbecile would want to take on China. But it's amazing how enthusiastic Australia gives its contemplation of war with China. And the only reason Australia's involved is because they've been promised a slice of the pie when it's all over to reconstruct the country. The same with Ukraine. Australia is not there for freedom or democracy. They're there because what they have been promised is a series of contracts for reconstruction. So, what you have for Australian Russians particularly children who are getting bullied in schools because they're Russian, and even though they are Australian, because they're Russian, it's all to benefit a small number of corporations in Australia. They have been promised contracts once this is all over and this is not democracy; this is just a nightmare scenario.

Hrvoje: You brought up the West and you know, this is one of, like, the top three things on my mind...More and more people I respect, they're starting to discuss. It's like a crescendo. You know, Paul Craig Roberts, I mentioned the other day, who's been a guest of mine. He just posted this week. *'The US is rapidly becoming an oppressive totalitarian society.'* John Leake, who's co-authored with Peter McCullough on his Substack, says he fears that the current regime will eventually obtain public dictatorial power and on and on it goes. I talked to other people I had online last night. Some experts are more optimistic. That feels like we're going to succeed in pushing back. What's your feeling?

Michael: I agree. I'm writing a new book, if I'm able to write it, called *Journey to the Forbidden Land* because we weren't allowed to visit here, we weren't allowed to visit. There are so many restrictions on banking you can't even get currency. You have to come here with Euros or US dollars and then exchange them across the border, but the government says you're not allowed to visit. *'Russia is too dangerous, but you can visit places like Ukraine.'* So, there's all these bizarre things that are happening, but I do agree. I think that someone wrote a book, if I can remember the title, I think it was Capitalism, Socialism and Democracy. He was looking at the different ideologies at the time. But I believe where we're heading to is a contest between only two. One is autocracy or a form of autocracy or whatever word you'd like to call it and fascism. There won't be any democracy. That's where we're heading. We're heading towards this great conflict between fascism and autocracy. And tragically, what's happened is that democracy, for whatever reason, has a cancer within it, which is its propensity to head towards neo-fascism or corporatism or whatever you want to call it and what I find interesting for if you go to the Trotskyites they're doing a lot of work on Ukraine and a few other topics and if you go to libertarians on the other side, you have the far left, the far right, they all agree that America is a fascist state, and they've said this for years, and they affirmed this conviction. You can put aside all the other things that the fascists believe, the libertarians, the Marxists, disagree with. But what's interesting is you have both sides who agree that there's something definitely wrong with the Imperium within the American Imperial system and it could be, the negative decline since the 1970s, definitely the declines for the systems and the filtering of the social consensus for democracy, focused on the idea of democracy is gone, and I think that the tragedy of Trump was that he actually believed he was President and he probably was the 1st president in a long time who actually thought he was President because the President is a puppet of the corporate interest who run the country. Trump's problem was he actually believed the Constitution and believed that he did have these rights, whereas in fact the people who are around him knew that those rights were bought a long time ago and we see this in this bizarre connection with Ukraine. Why Ukraine?

Hrvoje: If you could hold that thought. Have to come to our break. I did also want to go back to Ukraine for a second, but I would totally agree with you. I realized this early on that America has had for the longest time, fascism underneath the skin. And many people don't realize this, Americans, even in Western Europe, I mean. The EU is a fascist project and people don't want to hear it. They don't want to hear it. They'll yell at you. It's like Plato's Cave, you know, the analogy and so. Alright. Michael's website is freedommatterstoday.com. We'll be right back.

Hrvoje: It's our last segment with Michael Sutton, who's usually down under, but he just happens to, you know, happens to be going for a stroll at somewhere in Russia, which is fascinating.

His website is freedommatterstoday.com. Check it out. I listened to his latest podcast earlier today and very much enjoyed it, and I did have, I think I have a slight disagreement. But before maybe getting to that just to get your thoughts on the Ukraine situation, someone here in Mexico, I recently met a Ukrainian and she basically hates, you know, she's a young Ukrainian she hates the Russians, Russia so she has that classic, you know, sentiment, you know, as the Croats might have had in the early 90s and the Serbs with each other. But then I mentioned the fact that in 2008 Russia, in the Georgia War, that Georgia invaded Russia. And she was shocked. She got slightly perturbed. And I'm like, well, the EU actually has a report that says, *'Yes, Georgia did it.'* And we know that it was NATO that used Georgia as a puppet to start the war with Russia. But even Ukrainians who are at the center of the conflict, you know there's a problem with the emotions, right? You can't see clearly and then you know, this is often the case and so she got angry and so and I'm not on either side, I'm like looking at the facts. The fact was Georgia invaded Russia in 2008 and so still to this day, yeah, even people on Ground Zero, it's a fog of war. They don't even know. Still, don't know what's going on, even if you're a Ukrainian, in Ukraine. And so, I thought that was just an interesting anecdote. And do you have any thoughts on the wider war, where this might lead us, Poland is bringing troops to the, you know, to the Belarusian border. It just seems to think like things are expanding. You know, Kim Jong-un is prepping for war. And do you have any thoughts on NATO, Putin, Zelensky Ukraine and all that?

Michael: Yeah. Well, they were putting on Russian news yesterday, they were reporting on the Western reporting of the war and there seems to be a lot of acceptance of what they were saying a few months ago that the counter offensive was faltering. Which is fairly obvious, but I think the *'Stand with Ukraine'* is a simple scam promoted by corporations. And it is, in fact, when you look at what was really going on, what's the real motivation in the West it is the largest arms sale history, of live weapons testing in the towns, and villages in Ukraine. The West doesn't really care about these towns they've been wanting to test these weapons for years, and if you look at what's being tested by the Americans and Europeans, there's almost every weapon that they've made in the last 30 years, even Australia, which is scandalous for giving trucks that were only sent to Ukraine to be tested against Russian tanks and missiles. And I think what behind it is the fact the corporations were very content in Afghanistan for 20 years, and it was a bonanza. They were making a fortune for 20 years in this war, which they couldn't win against the Taliban. And then suddenly, the Americans pull out of Afghanistan. And so, these corporations have been looking around for another war ever since. And so, when Putin realized that the Europeans had betrayed them with the accords, then we have this conflict. But I think there is also Biden as well and as you know Biden and his family were involved with Ukraine throughout his vice presidency and now, currently there's all these allegations, that he's mired in allegations of corruption, his family, there's some bizarre connection with Joe Biden and Ukraine, which I believe is probably one of the reasons why there's such enthusiasm. They want to get conflict in Ukraine, and it is to reelect Joe Biden in 2024 and the awful things is that the people in Ukraine are suffering because of Joe Biden's desire to be President again. And so that's really what it's about. And it's interesting. I've already said there's more openness about UFOs in America than there is about Joe Biden's connections to Ukraine. And I think that tells you a lot about really what we were talking about before with the increasing fascism.

And yet there's allegations of Biden's corruption that that have been floating around for years that are just dismissed out of hand. He is the luckiest president in history. He could probably do anything he likes. The media will never report on it. And yet Trump is being indicted, left, right and center, in a farce which is undermining the American rule of law which they don't realize what they're doing, they're actually undermining the legal system. I think its persecution of a political candidate who is running for elections in the United States. So, I do believe that the key to the Ukraine crisis is tied to the persecution of a political candidate who's running for election in the United States. I do believe that the key to the Ukraine situation isn't freedom, freedom, Ukrainian freedom. But it has to do with the American ruling class and their contest of who's in Power 2024. Hillary Clinton, said she'd go to war with Russia when she got elected. Trump got elected and there was no war with Russia. Trump was defeated, and now there is conflict with Russia, and it's a sad day when the country doesn't exist without creating some kind of enemy. Surely democracy can stand on its own two feet with its own integrity.

Hrvoje: OK. Yeah, that's right. There's a there's a bit of a dropout with the with the zoom and delay, but you know it's still pretty magnificent that we can talk between Mexico and Russia via Australia, and I agree with you. I didn't think of that. I think there is, as you mentioned, there is a big focus on the military industrial complex and the money makers. It makes perfect sense for Afghanistan and now they move it to Ukraine, and you know Mexico. Abrams put out an article, I follow him, on Newsweek, that was mentioned on Ron Paul's Liberty Report. Does Ukraine have compromise on Joe Biden and the conclusion is despite the evidence of Biden's corruption, the Zelensky government has not outed Joe for his sordid history in this country. Why would Zelensky need to expose Biden and the tremendous American cost? Biden is leading the largest war since World War 2 to help Ukraine. Yet as American public support for it dries up, one cannot help but wonder how much freedom Biden has to step back from the war effort even if he wants to because Ukraine has the goods on Biden. And so, we only got a couple minutes left. Any other thoughts for us?

Michael: Well, I was wondering about what your thoughts on the podcast were.

Hrvoje:...You're talking more about Christianity, the church, and I mean, for the large part. I agree with it. You know, the church, as you mentioned, gets it wrong often and for me it's like that. The point is you don't throw the baby out with the bathwater, because man is sinful, you know, even believers and we make so many errors and so do our institutions, government institutions and churches. But you know the power that keeps us going there is Christ and the Holy Spirit and they make sure we don't fall completely off track. But then you mentioned why there's so many denominations we can't get our act together. That, you know, churches should pay taxes. I would agree. You know, that's the whole story you know, giving to Caesar and that they tend to be controlling because leaders tend to have ego and narcissism. You know, its fine, it's a struggle. And so, you know, you make a lot of great points. The one thing that I think I heard you say, you know, you say, *'don't go to church.'* And though I'm of the firm belief where it says believers should gather. So, I kind of do believe that you should participate in local church so any thoughts on that?

Michael: I was talking with this priest, this orthodox priest. I asked him. We were talking about the future of Orthodoxy in Russian, I asked what the main contribution of the Orthodox Church to Christianity is, and he said two things, hospitality, and love, and I thought that really sums up the Christian message, and I think if we can, if we can be people of hospitality, can be people of love, then this, then this can overcome all the challenges we face today, particularly hospitality. And the Russians are very good at hospitality, and we can learn a lot from that because it's really bringing people into your home, sharing a meal with them, talking with them, even though there are a lot of language barriers with Russians, their English is not very good, but they have still been very hospitable and this is, this is what the Christian faith is about. It's about showing kindness and love and being hospitable. And you never know, you might entertain an Angel unawares, as the Bible says and so I think that's really what I've learned a lot from my time in Russia.

Hrvoje: Yes. And you know, as you said that they are very hospitable, and they do tend to push a lot of vodka. So, you have the camera but dodge the vodka. The vodka bottle, so that's an interesting conversation but sometimes it becomes hard to say no. Alright real quick, 40 seconds left. Where do we best go to find your stuff online?

Michael: Keep an eye out for my books. I've written the

book, Baby Race, which looks at eugenics and population policies. My next book, *Journey to the Forbidden Lands* will be available in December, looking at Russia from Peter the Great, so keep an eye for that and thank you so much very much for being on the show.

Hrvoje: Great, you too, great to get an update.

6

25 SEPTEMBER 2023

Interview with Neil Johnson, 20Twenty Vision Podcast, Vision Christian Media

Topics: Russia, the West, Ukraine, truth, propaganda, faith.

https://omny.fm/shows/20twenty/russia-and-the-freedoms-of-the-west-michael-sutton

TRANSCRIPT

Neil: We are talking about Russia, we're going to be talking about the West because Australia, one of those Western nations, we're going to talk about our freedoms, freedom of speech, you know, the idea that you and I can think believe, analyze facts converse with others, communicate our thoughts and feelings, through spoken or written word, it's been a founding principle of our modern Western democracies. It allows individuals to question established beliefs, narratives, and ideas, including government policies. Well, our special guest today recently returned from a trip to Russia, and he's started asking questions about the state of our world, including our personal freedoms in the West, Dr. Michael Sutton is writing a book on Russia. It's called, *'Journey to the Forbidden Land,'* and he's revising his book, which is called, *'Is Russia Our Enemy?'* a study of Christ's defeat of our true enemy, Satan. Dr. Michael Sutton is a political economist, a professor, a pastor. He's now a publisher and back with us once again today, Michael Sutton, a special welcome back to 2020.

Michael: Oh, thank you very much, Neil. It's so wonderful to be with you again. Thank you very much.

Neil: And Michael, upon your return from Russia, you've written a thought-provoking article too that was published by the Brownstone Institute, called, *'A Letter from a Forbidden Land.'* You better take us into this. Tell us about your visit. Some of us might even be surprised that you can actually visit Russia in this day and age. What are your thoughts? Give us your story.

Michael: Well, the government doesn't want us to visit

Russia. You know, you can go to the DFAT web page, they'll tell you that you shouldn't go to Russia. But it's a bit of a problem for the many thousands of Russian Australians who live here and their families and friends and people who just want to visit. You can't get travel insurance from Australia, and you can't have currency exchange, but when you get to Russia you find it's a remarkable place. It's a beautiful country. It's a vast country. I think that's what strikes you. It's a vast nation. We caught the Trans-Siberian Railway across half of the country and what's remarkable about Russia is it's a very multiethnic and also multi religious society. There are laws prohibiting, I guess, the proselytizing of people across those kinds of religious boundaries which is understandable in the country. It has a very large Buddhist and Muslim population and a Christian population. But what struck me when I was in Moscow standing on the bridge in front of the largest cathedral in Russia that was built after the Cold War ended, that there were churches almost everywhere and everywhere around Russia. There was a church that was built on an old bus station. And through which a number of people came to Christ and people remember that *'Oh, that's the church at the bus station,'* and they have chapels in their parks, chapels in universities, and university professors can go and pray after their lectures.

And so, what you saw in Russia is they have had under

Lenin, but particularly through Stalin, an appalling persecution of Christians and Christians were forbidden to practice their faith. Millions were sent to the gulags and so on, but what they did, the Christians who were not killed or put in prison, they internalized their faith, they made it their own. They held onto their faith, and it became a real personal faith in God and Christ. There are the Old Believers, and they're very devout people, very sincere followers of Christ, and they have built these communities and these towns where they practice their faith. And then there's another strand of Christianity in Russia, which is an internal faith of a personal faith where they don't follow a particular church building or church organization, but they follow Christ. They follow God in their own way, something like the non-church movement in Japan. So, this is pretty much a thread, several threads of Christianity in Russia. When you think of it, the Christians are very open about talking about their lives, and I mean everyone's aware of the conflict in the Ukraine and they're aware of the origins of the conflict dating back to 2014, when America helped to topple the democratically elected government in Ukraine and put in their puppet. And then, you know, and you see it on Zelensky's face, he's like a kite in a whirlwind. He doesn't know whether he's coming or going. You see little glimpses of Zelensky at the United Nations where he says his opinion publicly and everyone condemns him and my great fear with this whole situation is that America would betray the Ukraine like they've betrayed the Kurds. And we will just move on and onto the next conflict which may be in Africa, maybe climate change, ultimately, what needs to happen is there needs to be peace, a settlement, negotiation. Sadly, the churches are aiming for total defeat of Russia, which will not happen. Russia will prevail in this conflict. They just simply have more factories. It is like the Civil War in America, the North won because they had the factories and Russia will win because they have the factories and the weapons. Doesn't matter how many Abrams tanks America sends them.

Neil: A few things that are inconsistent with the sorts of impressions that might be left in your heart and mind around who the true enemy is. When we look at all of the different conflicts, but we are getting a bit of a focus today on Russia and the Ukraine conflict, our special guest. Dr. Michael Sutton has just returned from a visit to Russia where religious freedom, the church in Russia, is flourishing in a level of freedom they've perhaps not been used to, and yet there are some rising issues that we have in the West that's putting lots of our freedoms under threat. Michael, we will take some calls shortly, but on this issue so far as the Western nations and Australia, it's a Western nation. We have seen lots of our own freedoms coming under threat. Your reflections here from your visit to Russia and thoughts about some rising threats here.

Neil: Yeah, no, absolutely, Neil. I think what really struck me in the West, I had this privilege of meeting this family who were living in Russia. And she told me, the wife told me the story of her grandmother, and she lived in, I think was Belarus before the war, it was part of the old Soviet Union, there's a guy in their town who didn't like them because they had a cow and so he went to the KGB and reported on them to the KGB in those days, and reported on them that they were enemies of the state. And so, they were then persecuted. They had children and they had to forcibly move from one side of Russia to the other, and this lady had great faith in Jesus, and they went, and they lost their kids, all their kids perished. And then they reestablished in the middle of Russia in the Ural Mountains, and they built a life for themselves. They were very successful, God blessed them in their lives and they, and all their children were successful. And then at the end of their life, they went back to that old town and there was almost no one left in that town, except the man who was their Judas, who had betrayed them, and they went to him and asked him, *'was it worth it?'* And he just looked at them, in horror that they were still alive. And for me, it was a real great story of faith, the grandmother used to say, *'the Lord God will lead me, the Lord God will lead me.'* So, despite all the persecution under Stalin, she still had her faith within her. And yet the terrible things happened because this man didn't like them. He made up an accusation and they got persecuted and that's where we are today in the West and that's what we are entering into at the moment, you have these soldiers who are going off to fight for freedom in the Ukraine against Russia and when they come back they might be prosecuted cancelled or sued if they say something as radical, as *'only women can get pregnant,'* or *'Christ is Lord.'* Or things that we used to say every day, but now we're not allowed to say. And so, what we're seeing in Russia and in China is we're seeing that they went through hell. But the Maoist period was a nightmare, the Stalinist period was a nightmare, but God's people are resurrected. He has people in those places, and so whatever future they have, they are not gonna have the nightmare that God has in store for us because the future of Australia has a lot of your listeners will know is that free speech is under attack, democracy is under attack, like never before, unlike anything we've ever seen, particularly in Covid Hysteria where they shut down, everything, closed down the churches, now we're being told with the this so called Referendum, you must vote, *'yes.'* You don't see many no votes, no placards around, because people will get persecuted if they express their opinion so, I mean so where is the better place to live, in a country like Russia or in

Australia, where persecution looks like it's just around the corner?

Neil: There are controversial elements to a conversation like this, and it may be raising some issues for you. Well, our Talkback line is open. Let's take a call. Alex is in Melbourne. Hi, Alex. Welcome along.

Listener: Hello and you're welcome back, yes. I'm a bit confused. I heard on Vision News maybe a week or two ago there was a pastor from a Baptist pastor from Russia had to leave Russia. I think his name was Yuri Sitko. I think was mentioned on the news, and I thought, well I'm not too sure whether he was praying for both Russia and Ukraine, or well, what the situation was doesn't make sense.

Neil: It doesn't make sense and I'll get Michael in on this because when you hear these sorts of stories and there are pastors who are outspoken, I guess it's one thing to be allowed to flourish in freedom, but if you do say the wrong thing that rubs up against the regime, then you are going to be in trouble, aren't you? So, a thought or two from Michael.

Michael: Well, if you read my book, very controversial book *'Is God on America's side?'* I take issue with the whole idea of free speech because from the Christian viewpoint, there really is no such thing as free speech because you know, James says that our tongue is like a raging fire. And what we say can build or destroy, discourage, encourage, or discourage, and so we are encouraged to be very careful how we speak and there are lots of laws around what we can and can't say anyway, even in our free society, you can't slander anyone, you can't, you know, make up stories about people, and it astounds me, you know, like, the very rich people like Hillary Clinton and the people like them have horrible things have been said about them by so many people, and they just choose not to sue people because but it's entirely their right to do so. There are restrictions in Australia on what we can and can't say, and they're there for very good reason. Every country is different. Every country has different rules about what you can and can't say. I mean, I reflect on Saint Paul where he talks about Christ is Lord. And yet whenever he said, *'Christ as Lord,'* that was an affront to the Roman Empire. But at the same time, he used his Russian, not Russian, he used his Roman citizenship to advance the gospel. So, it's a complex kind of world we live in. I think we have to find the light in the dark places, and we have to maneuver as God sees us.

Neil: Alex in Melbourne. Anything more to add, Alex?

Listener: Oh well, I'm pretty sure that Russian Orthodox would do their best to be on the side of Putin, but anyway, I don't know. I just like to read the word of God, because that's the real light in there and real freedom is in the Lord

Jesus Christ. God help us.

Neil: Alex, thanks so much for your contribution. Our Talkback line is open. Interesting to raise this because in my understanding and you might have some other insight here, Michael, while in the West we still have in many instances separation of church and state. In other words, the state does not have control over the church. From what I understand, in Russia the Russian Orthodox Church is under the founder of the Communist Party under Putin and they do have some right of veto over who is appointed as a Bishop or an Archbishop. Any thoughts you got about a minute to news time.

Michael: I agree with Alex, that freedom comes through Christ, and Alex is absolutely right, our freedom is in Jesus Christ. But there's no Communist Party in Russia as I, as I understand it, Putin's not a not a communist but, but the West doesn't have separation of church and state. We've never had that; we have churches that survive through tax exemptions. They survived through whatever the state decides for them, and there's strong relationships between the churches, education system and government policy. So, it's not really a strict, we're not the United States. We don't have that strict separation of church and state in Australia.

Neil: Why don't we take some calls from listeners? Let's hear from Katie, who is in Victoria. Hi Katie. Welcome along. Are you well, Katie, what are your thoughts?

Listener: Hi gentlemen, Yeah, sorry. I actually came in partly through the conversation. I heard something about it earlier and I was trying to avoid it because to be honest, I get anxiety and just stressed out even thinking about the way the Western countries are going, including Australia. So, I'll try and think about it. It's a little bit like to be honest. Because it upsets me. I don't wanna just speak about something, talking about privacy issues because we know that a lot of information is collected, you know, online on Facebook and Google and all that sort of stuff. But even on our phones...

Neil: Heidi, you're raising some important issues and there's certainly a way that this is a part of our conversation in some sense, and let's come to our guest today, Dr. Michael Sutton, because all this information gathering, our privacy issues, our freedom issues, our surveillance issues, and this is what I think Katie is referring to, no one is safe, around questions of privacy and freedom, and there's always that risk that those things that are said in the past and they're on the record digitally by way of our data and our metadata, those can be used against us. And this would be something that we'd often refer to as happening in nations like Russia or in China, where surveillance is so significant that this is the way that the government controls the people. Any thoughts here for Katie?

Michael: Well, the difference between this is a really

good question, Katie is it's a bit from left field but it's very it's very important, we have in societies we need something to hold them together. So, in an authoritarian society you need force, usually force or the rule of law is very important and so, people fall out of line, they go to prison. So, it's force that holds them together in authoritarian states. But in societies like Australia, which at least claims to be a democracy, what holds society together is propaganda and propaganda is essentially persuasion. We're encouraged to behave in certain ways and is indicative of, I guess decline in the government's belief that people are good, we see the rise in the surveillance state in the West, and so we see a greater paranoia. The paranoia is in the US, the paranoia is in the government, and we see it there. They're dumbing down the population through social media. They want to make us as stupid as possible as dumb as possible, because the greatest human resource is you Katie and like everyone else who listens. Because God's given us a brain which is the most amazing thing ever created by God and governments in the West, they don't want us to use that brain. They want us to just do as we're told, and so it's probably a reflection, I think of the government, certainly since 9/11, the government in the West, they're declining faith in their own people to trust them, trust them to believe in a certain way, behave in a certain way. And this happened a century ago as well, this crisis of confidence within the government. If you go back to the beginning decade of the 20th century, the great fear was what happened in Russia, with the Russian Revolution, terrible fear over that, that this might happen in America or Australia. And so, as a result of that was the welfare state to, I guess, placate the poor, and prevent them from rising up against the government. And so, we've had the welfare state for 100 years and so, we're coming towards the end of this period. And so, there's this rising paranoia of the government. So, I think you've really hit the nail on the head there, Katie, and how we, how we go from there. Well, that's another question entirely.

Neil: Maybe anything further to add?

Listener: Ah, no, I just I. Just think it's really sad. It's just like it breaks my heart. It's great that you, you're all talking about it, and we do have to keep, you know, seeking to try and do God's will every day and serve the Lord even if things become really difficult. I mean, even if you know, even if we go to jail for our faith, because I think that's, I mean that's where a lot of this is heading, and you know, we're just hopefully, well, we know that the Lord's coming soon, and we need to try and keep our eyes fixed on. Jesus and I think that that's all we need to do as individual believers.

Neil: Well, done, Katie. Katie, thank you so much for your call. Our Talkback line is open. Let's just stay with this for a moment and just put you into a little corner here, Michael put you on the spot. As Christians, we appreciate the gospel message, there is a proclamation of that message. As some people would say that over many centuries of the church, the church has been a little bit coercive and even propaganda oriented as well. The difference between this proclamation and propaganda, I mean as Christians, we have this proclamation of the gospel. There is a narrative around God's revealed way of seeing things, believing things. But you've got this propaganda that's coming from some of these coercive authoritarian states, and they're growing here in Australia too. Any thoughts here around the thoughts of propaganda and coercion and who we put our trust and faith in.

Michael: I think that's a really good question, Neil. I think that what you have increasingly since 911 probably is an increasing, I guess we've adopted a lot of American thinking about politics and about the world and we've kind of been sucked in like a vacuum cleaner, it has sucked us into the American culture war, so you have a lot of Christians talking about the left wing view of the Communist view and in Communist China, there's no Communism in China, it is long gone, it's the socialist market economy or there's the Right view, that Christians can't be Left, they can't have a Left-Wing view they must be Right Wing. I always like to say that there's the view on the Right and a view on the Left and then there is the truth. And the truth always comes from the scriptures, that's God's word to us. And I think I'd encourage your readers to open the Bible and read the Bible and let God speak through his Word what he wants to say to them with that particular day and God says that he will give you wisdom if they ask for it, if they want it and the answers to all our problems are there in the scriptures that God has promised to us, but there are a lot of things he doesn't promise to us. He doesn't promise, you know, nice sports cars and nice houses. But he does give us his Son, and in in the Son there is freedom, there's life and there's reconciliation to God. So, everything we need in life is found in the Son, and we must follow him wherever that wherever that leads.

Neil: Of course, it's an interesting conversation, isn't it, to talk about how you establish and understand the truth of it's all very well to say, open the Bible and truth will be there. But there is a certain discernment of how that truth applies to all of the circumstances that we might be trying to assess the issues of a nation and focuses the need of the issues that a family or a community focuses on, and discerning the truth and I guess some of those things you boil down to some rules of thumb that what a Christian believes. And as you say, not necessarily right or left, but how do we discern truth out of what God says. Now let me just put you on the spot again here. Michael, because there's other big issues that we're talking about now and you know the last caller who called through Katie, I mean, she was saying, you know, things like, you know, dumbing down and the surveillance idea of trying to control people. Is there something here that we can talk around, perhaps even, you know? What is one of the most relevant issues to Australians right now? The Voice we're going to be asked to vote yes or no on the 14th of October. Some will say there's been a huge dumbing down of trying to understand what that might mean. Now give us your insights here into how you make use of the sentiment, perhaps using the Voice as an example.

Michael: OK, well, your listeners might be interested in the subject for today's podcast in my series, which is what is God's opinion of the Voice which was available today on Spotify and freedommatterstoday.com. But I was reflecting on what Katie mentioned looking under Jesus, the author of our faith. I think she was quoting from Hebrews there and I'm starting a new series where I'm going through Hebrews and looking at who is Jesus, the nature of Jesus and I keep coming back when I'm thinking about the Voice to that first chapter, where it says long ago God spoke many times in many ways to our ancestors through the prophets, and now in these final days he has spoken to us through his Son. So, for me, the voice, the only voice that matters, is the voice of God through the Son. And so, we need to dwell on the identity, the words, the actions of Christ, and when we've run out of time, looking at that, we should look at it again. For me, God gives us a brain and he's given us reason, and we ultimately for decisions of politics, we must make up our own mind on these things. I remember there was a famous Australian politician who was asked his opinion on some topic, and he said this was his decision and he was, look, I'm a Christian, I follow Jesus, but I'm approaching this issue from my understanding of politics and there's nothing wrong with that. There's nothing wrong with a man or a woman wanting to be a soldier, for example, going to an honorable profession. God honors the men in Russia who are fighting for Russia, the ones who are fighting for Ukraine. He honors men and women who decide to serve their country, but he doesn't tell us which side he's on in a war. Nowhere in Scripture does he say he's on the side of the Left or the Right, or the up or the down, that those things are hidden from us. And it's a good thing because if we knew that God was on the side or a particular side of battle, we would know that the deaths of those men and women was intentional and that's not how God works. God gives us freedom. He honors the day, and his mysteries are in those sort of everyday providential things are hidden from our sight, but he's given us wisdom to make that decision. Whether we should vote yes or no, but we should not listen to those who say. *'Only Christians should vote yes or only Christians should vote no,'* because those people don't know who God is, I'm really sorry. Those guys who are saying yes or no from this is what God says. Well, God's view is that I want you to listen to my Son. That's God's view. And As for the other things in life? He's given us reason; he's given us intelligence to make up our own mind. And anyone who tells you otherwise, just give them a copy of the gospels.

Neil: OK. Well, we're talking Russia. We've also introduced now some conversation around what happens when there is propaganda, when there is a dumbing down, where there are power and control issues. Let's take another call. Glenn is in Serena in Queensland. Hi, Glenn. Welcome along.

Listener: Hi, Neil. How are you doing? Thanks, guys, for your work. Thank you.

Neil: And what are your thoughts today?

Listener: Just wanted to contribute, but perhaps. A little insight on my ex-soldier. I served in the Australian army. For 20 years regular army. Perhaps the way our brothers and sisters could view our current world, if they look back at history, if you could consider there's been a number of world empires. And it's important to remember that during World War 2, Russia was actually our ally against the Nazis in that particular conflict. In my opinion, with the five other nations, and from what I've seen it might be a different way to look at the current political landscape, to view the West as the current world empire and perhaps Australia could be considered the southern province of the empire, and any empire likes to flex its muscle, it doesn't like to be defeated, it likes to push its agenda, so I just like to put that thought forward and perhaps our listeners could say, *'Hey, I. Never thought of it like that we live in a democratic country also, we're told, but what's interesting? Is that it doesn't matter how people vote. The direction continues to go on the same line, and we seem to change the jockey, but not get rid of the horse.'*

Neil: I think there's real wisdom in the things you're sharing here, Glenn, because it all seems to me that everyone's on one side here. And so, when we're talking Left and Right and where the Christian discerns truth in all of that, that gets to be challenging.

Michael: Well, thank you, Glenn, for your service for our country, it's always an amazing thing for those who decide to join the armed forces and serve their country is a great thing regardless of which flag they fight under, there's a real camaraderie there and I think what you say you're absolutely right that Australia as part of the American empire. We were part of the British Empire for a long time. I, say controversially in my article, Australia was a mercenary state. We seem to fight many wars that other people want us to fight. In this particular conflict, one of the reasons Australia is in the conflict is for the promised bounty that we'll get once the conflict is over, in terms of military contracts and reconstruction contracts. We have contracts with American corporations, but we gave away a lot of bushmasters and stuff for free to the Ukraine, which was bizarre without any strings attached. What's interesting is, as you say, it is an empire, and we are in a place where we have so many Christians in Australia. And Jesus said, blessed are the peacemakers, for they shall be called children of God, and for many Christians, however, they just follow whichever war the government wants, and as a result of this, Christian faith declines. It's interesting in the Soviet Union. I saw footage of what they did. There's an incredible museum in Ekaterinburg, a beautiful museum about Russia and it's a video museum and held this footage about the Russian state's approach to the church. It's unbelievable because they blew them up. They just blew them up, exploding the churches church after church, and put thousands of ministers in prison. But, through that experience they held onto their faith and they, and as a result of that today, Russia is a country where people, you know, they are increasingly free to, to practice their faith, what's happening in Australia because Christians ought to stand up for what the gospel is about, which is peace from God, but also peace between ourselves. And we don't have any human enemy. As Paul says, we don't wrestle against flesh and blood, but against principalities and powers. But even though we do wrestle against Satan, Satan as defeated by Christ in the wilderness and at the Cross, and his goal today is to destroy the testimony of Christ amongst the faithful, and we have to keep going back to what Jesus has done for us.

Neil: Liam, thank you so much for your call and time is running short. Let's squeeze in one more call. Julie is in Robina on the Gold Coast in QLD. Hi Julie, welcome.

Listener: Hi, thank you. I haven't heard that thing on how so I can hear the radio, but just while we're the direction and headed, but you had been talking about but mainly the war with Russia and Ukraine and all that sort of thing, and now I am in my 60s and yeah, I've been horrified with the way Australia is heading of late with freedom of speech and propaganda being spread, and if it's something different than the government believes then, you know, misinformation and all that sort of thing. So. You know, to me that's been alarming. Had that been able to happen in our country and, you know, laws come in against freedom of speech and all that sort of thing.

But I suppose my question is the war with Russia and Ukraine and you know, with the comment was nice that you know we don't really know on which side God is and that sort of thing, but I suppose, and I only know what they said to us too so many violations of human rights. And I suppose, you know, I have to ask myself, if a leader of a country is allowed that sort of thing that, think we're quite widespread in that war how could we, justly respond you know, it's good that Christians are having more of a free reign there, but...

Neil: Julie, I think it making some good points here just to pick up on this thought and get Michael's insight here because in the context of our conversation, wherever there are those dreadful violations of human rights, Christians ought to be perhaps speaking up for those who can't speak for themselves. Any thoughts here for the things Julie is saying, Michael and this thought that you know, whose side are you on? Well, we're on God's side. But I thought lets hear for the sorts of things Julie is sharing.

Michael: Yeah, absolutely, Julie. Well, it's sort of two-way conflict. I mean, there are human rights abuses against the peoples of the Donetsk as well. I mean there is a family here in Australia who had a beautiful home in Ukraine, and it was going well, and the Ukrainians blew their house to bits, destroyed their home, and now they're living in Australia as refugees. And so, they have been here for, for quite a while. This is well before the conflict escalated in 2022. So, the war's been going on for almost 10 years now. And when I was in Russia, they also have the pictures of the children of one of these towns where they were stuck under the house, their parents basically put them underneath the house for eight years because their town was being bombed by Ukraine for eight years. But we don't hear about any of that. We just hear about whatever the American media wants us to hear about in the western media about the one-sided conflict. I mean, both sides have been accused of war crimes and war is a horrible thing, and maybe I think the answer would have been if America hadn't stopped rearming or arming Ukraine after February 2222 there would have a peace settlement and maybe the Americans and the Western powers who didn't renege on the Minsk Agreement in 2014, which they signed in 2015, in 2022 in, in February, then then we wouldn't be in this conflict as well as we know from the Germans, the Germans admitted that the Minsk agreement was in fact a farce and they intended to arm Ukraine in the intervening years. And so, America actually had military personnel on the ground in Ukraine before this conflict began. So, what were they doing there? And we mustn't also forget the 130 bio labs that the Americans have in the Ukraine as well. So, we're gonna ask a question. What are they doing there as well? So, geopolitics is a messy business. I would go back to what Glenn was saying. God honors the soldiers and he doesn't you know, he honors the soldiers of both sides and he knows where they from and he knows their lives in their last moments and he holds them in his heart, even when we forget them. And for me, as someone who's been involved with RSL and that we forget the most important lesson of war. It isn't the war, but it's what happens afterwards, and we have to, we can never forget the soldiers who fight. We can never forget them, and we should always support them. Doesn't matter what side they're on because they are often the ones we neglect.

Neil: And there are thousands of soldiers who have lost their lives in this dreadful conflict. Thank you so much Julie for your insight. Time has run out for listeners who want to connect with our guest today. Dr. Michael Sutton, political economist and professor, pastor, publisher his website is freedommatterstoday.com. You'll be able to have a listen in for his thoughts around the Voice on his podcast today, you're also able to connect with Michael through not only his website, but he has just published *'A Letter from the Forbidden Land.'* with the Brownstone Institute. Brownstone.org is the website there. He's written a number of books. We talked about *'Is Russia our enemy?'* that has been re-released. Michael's also writing a book called *Journey to the Forbidden Land.* Last time we were talking, we were talking about a book that he'd written called *Freedom from Fascism, A Christian Response to Mass Formation Psychosis.* As I'm going to get into some deep stuff, look into those, at freedommatterstoday.com.

Dr. Michael Sutton, thank you so much for taking some time to share your thoughts and your insights with listeners today on 20/20.

Michael: Thank you very much, Neil. It's been a wonderful privilege to be on. Thank you very much. God bless you.

7

1 OCTOBER 2023

Emeritus Professor Reuben Ross's 'Sons of Issachar,' podcast, 'Freedom Matters,' Podcast Episode

https://reubenrose.substack.com/p/freedom-matters-podcast

Topics: Covid Theology, biography, freedom, Covid Hysteria, Government overreach, Fascism, Propaganda.

TRANSCRIPT

Reuben: Freedom and faith are intertwined and have been at the heart of many physical and spiritual struggles over the millennia. We need to take freedom seriously and understand that it is an unalienable right given by God. And not something bestowed by governments. Now as I contemplated some of the challenges, we face in relation to freedom over these many months, I was delighted and surprised to find a provocative article called *'Covid Theology in the Australian Church,'* which was published by the Brownstone Institute in February this year. The article was drawn to my attention by a friend and the post was written by Dr. Michael J. Sutton, a political economist, professor, priest, pastor, and publisher. In the newsletter I've got a link to his articles. Dr. Sutton wrote this in his article about the Church's response to Covid. And I'm just quoting from that article called Covid Theology in the Australian Church. Here's what Dr. Sutton wrote back in February and published:

'By closing the church door to the unvaccinated, many were embracing a malicious apostasy that we have not seen since Franco. From July 2021 to mid-2022, vaccine passports were used in churches loyal to the state. What it meant was someone could go to church with the flu, hepatitis, syphilis, herpes and early onset of Ebola if they had their Covid vaccination certificate. Australian churches were enticed to behave corruptly. To sweeten the deal, thousands of religious practitioners during the Covid lockdowns receive financial rewards from the state. It was the largest direct transfer of direct funds to the church in

Australian history. The Christian Church is one of the most corrupt institutions in the West. It has been bathing its emaciated body in the oils of tax exemptions and special treatment for over a century. And as a result, is drowning in scandals, corruption, child abuse and nepotism."

It's the end of the quote. Such plain and writing is rare in our times, and I followed up to find that Dr. Sutton had written a book which I acquired a few months ago called Freedom from Fascism. And I've got a link to that book in the newsletter. I finished the book relatively recently and I think it's a great read and I can recommend that heartily to my readers. Its available on Amazon and in my 5- Star Amazon Review this is what I wrote. *"Michael Sutton is a brave and outspoken man who is much needed in these times when many have forgotten about the Covid tyranny and bio security overreach. As he indicates in this provocative book, it is impossible to be a Christian and let the government decide who has the right to hear the good news about God."*

Now, Michael also has written a number of other books, and I'm currently reading his interesting book called Baby Race, which deals with the complex issues around demographics and falling birth rates. I decided that it would be interesting for my Sons of Issachar readers and listeners to have the opportunity to hear Dr. Sutton. And so, in the last day or so I interviewed him for this podcast.

Interestingly, he's just returned from Russia and so next week I'm going to have a further interview about the situation in Russia at the moment. Dr. Sutton has a website called Freedom Matters Today, and I've got a link to that in the newsletter, but if you just type in freedom matters today, you'll find the website and all the details of these books are there. So here follows the interview with Doctor Michael Sutton.

Michael, welcome to the Sons of Issachar podcast. I'd like to introduce Dr. Michael Sutton, who is, I think, in the old terms, a polymath. He's got an interest in many things, and I came across him in an interesting post, from the Brownstone Institute, a US based website that's highlighted some of the challenges around Covid. And I saw an inflammatory post on the 3rd of February this year, brought to attention by a friend of mine. And I thought I like this guy. He's prepared to challenge the existing narrative and particularly to challenge the existing narrative in relation to the church. Michael describes himself in many ways. I'll just read from the back of his book. He's the founder and CEO of Freedom Matters Today, which looks at freedom from a Christian perspective. He's got a PhD from the University of Sydney and a Master of Divinity. And you've even got a Moore College Diploma, and Michael, it would be good to have a little bit of background about you from your own perspective that the sort of start of your life was really around political economics. And so, you and our current Prime Minister, Anthony Albanese have a lot in common. He also studied political economy. So, give us a little bit of your own story. And I know, as an aside, that you as quite a significant period of time in Japan. As well as in Washington DC, so some of your own background would be helpful for listeners, because I think we're going on a fascinating journey that might involve us doing 2 podcasts. Anyway, thank you for being with us.

Michael: It's a great privilege to be here, Ruben, and thank you very much for inviting me on and for also your kind welcome and introduction. I didn't think there would be something in common I had with Anthony Albanese but there you go. I'm not sure where he studied but I studied in Sydney and went to my local public school, which was great. I enjoyed that and it was a very good school, Jannali Boys High School. And then I went on to the University of Sydney and I studied economics as a social science or Political Economy, as it was called in those days, and I graduated first-class Honours. And then I went on to do a PhD in political economy and my dissertation was the Asia Pacific Economic Cooperation or APEC, as it was known in those days, I think is still with us. It has become, I guess, like all things bureaucratic, it has a life of its own and will continue forever until it is brought to an end. APEC, at the time I was writing and researching was supposed to be, I guess the vehicle for bringing China and America and Asia together in an economic way to promote peace through international trade, that certainly was the goal that was driven by the belief of many in the field of economics that international trade can dovetail itself with peace, and you can have a world where everyone benefits through economic growth and development. That was certainly the original vision.

Reuben: So, most of these international organizations have lost their goals. How would APEC differ from the goals of the WTO then?

Michael: The WTO is an institution created by the signatories of the world who decided to create it back in 1995, and the WTO World Trade Organization was what many had hoped would be the International Trade organization that was America's brainchild back in the 1940s. America proposed it and tried to promote the International Trade Organization to sit alongside the World Bank and International Monetary Fund. But after the war, there was a lot of protectionism in America, in Congress. And so, they decided to ditch the International Trade Organization, much to the surprise of everyone who had signed on to what the Americans wanted. And so, they were left with what was the General Agreement on Tariffs and Trade which oversaw the American trade system, which is the trade in goods and services increasingly and it was a useful agreement for many years and oversaw a number of what we call trade negotiations in the multilateral sphere, but by the 1970s there were so many issues arising in international trade that hitherto had not really been significant, such as technical barriers to trade, trade and services, trade and agriculture, trade and everything, really intellectual property investment, and so it was seen that the international trading system needed an institution, and so they created the World Trade Organization, which is an international body similar to the World Bank or the International Monetary Fund, and its goal is to, in a sense, oversee the maintenance of these international trade rules to do with mainly trading goods, trade and services. They don't look at investments so much. Intellectual property is another one. Technical barriers to trade, lots of other issues, but the WTO is still there and it's still functioning, but no government has the courage to start another trade around, and this has been the case for about 20 years.

Reuben: And one of the big changes happened when China was admitted, I think under the Clinton administration, wasn't it? The WTO and a lot of things changed internationally, but the I suppose the interesting story we could get in this line for quite a lot longer but it's not the focus of what we're going to cover today. I just wonder, in your own story, how did you move from that area, which I can see is fascinating into the area of theology and theological study and your own journey then into becoming a minister or an ordained minister? As far as I can understand, is that right, you're currently an ordained Minister of the church.

Michael: Ordained priest in the Anglican tradition.

Reuben: Right, so, tell me just about that, that interesting journey.

Michael: OK, I'm happy to. So, I went to Japan to further my academic studies in international trade policy, after I finished my PhD. And so, I continued with that. I worked for an organization that no longer exists, called the WTO Research Centre in Tokyo, which was a quasi-government. Institute, not surprisingly, looking at WTO issues and that was really a great experience for me under the leadership of Professor Iwata, who was a one of Japan's leading. WTO scholars. But by about 2008, having been in Japan for about ten years, I decided I spent enough time looking at international trade policy because there's only so much you could really investigate in this area until you've exhausted it. And I studied it for a very long time, and I thought I'd come to an end of it. But then at that particular time, there was a lot of talk in Japan over the low birthrate, and the idea that Japanese women needed to go back home and be barefoot and pregnant and have babies for the nation and they were betraying their nation, and they were looking after their own individual selfishness and self-interest and so on. And I was astounded by the statements coming from politicians whom I respected at the time because of their views on other things. But when it came to demographic policy, it was astoundingly stupid, most of the things they were talking about, and then I realized, well, this is an area that I should investigate. And it had actually been my first choice when I was considering projects for my dissertation, and so I was actually warned away from population policy because I was told that it's incredibly sensitive, controversial, it is likely to get you into a lot of trouble because of the nature of the subject. So, I took the advice of my then mentor who was at university and I went for trade policy, which is some would say a cure for insomnia.

Reuben: And you definitely made a difference. I have just been reading through your book. Michael's got a relatively new book called *'Baby Race'* that actually I realized has its genesis a long time ago. So, as you said when you were starting to become interested in this thing, this area and I suppose it's particularly interesting because Japan really has virtually no immigrants as it's a relatively close society compared with something like Western Europe or even Australia.

Michael: Well, Japan is similar to most western nations. It's not Western, of course, but it's similar to the most western developed countries. It has a low birth rate as I demonstrate in the book. But for some reason, scholars are obsessed with Japan, and they neglect the same, I guess the same dynamics occurring in Western European countries, which I find very strange in a way, because maybe it's because the academics are aboard, studying Europe and they might get a free trip to Japan if they start talking about how bad Japan is and so they go to Japan, have a good time to kill to write that article about how terrible Japan is. But what's happening in Japan is indicative of economic development, it's natural for countries that are prosperous to have lower birth rates. This is a perfectly natural process and also the fact that rate is as a result of contraception and other devices that we have created in recent years to prevent pregnancy. It's quite natural for birth rates to fall and the rise in technology supposes another feature in, I guess, destroying the need for old fashion industries which needed large labor forces anyway, so.

Reuben: How did that then take you from there to as opposed training and theology and being ordained as an Anglican priest.

Michael: Well, that's an interesting story. So, I went because of my studies on Japan's demographic change, economic and strategic implications of that. I was offered a position at the East West Centre in Washington DC because they were interested at the time. I guess that the population decline in Japan, Korea and Taiwan, which also those countries have low birth rates, particularly Taiwan and Korea, and then of course at the time they're looking at China, as at the time, the One Child Policy was still there still active. And so, I was invited there to give a talk and to do research on national demographic policy and so at the end of that went back to Australia and I was renovating a home with a friend of mine who was a Presbyterian minister. We were repairing one of those old-fashioned windows you know the old ones with the spring windows the old-fashioned windows they have in a lot of homes in Australia. It's a very complicated window. I can't remember the name of the particular type of window, but it has a spring, and you need, well, it's very complicated. Anyway, we're repairing this window, and he asked me, had I ever thought about being involved in Christian ministry. And it was like a light had turned on and I felt from that moment I was called to the ministry. I had a call to tell people about the good news of Jesus. I've always been a person who for as long as I can remember followed, Christ followed Jesus. I've had a deep sense and awareness of the presence of God in my life. I'm not afraid to nail my colors to the mast and say I'm a Christian and if people have a problem with that I don't care. There was a great Christian in the Sutherland Shire called Ieuan Lumsden and he was a great Christian man and mentor for many people. He also was a missionary in China before the communists took over and he always said to me, Michael, you have to nail your colors to the mast. You have to say you're a Christian, you have to make a stand and you have to put your faith out there. It can't just be a private thing. It's something that that the world must know, and the world must know that Jesus is Lord, and so, for me, that personal faith I had has been with me for a long time. My mother was important in my spiritual formation in the early days, as was my uncle and a number of other people.

Reuben: So, what an interesting story that around the focus on fixing a window and a complicated hinge that somehow God speaks in many unusual ways to us, but its undoubtedly true that when God speaks, you need to listen, and you need to follow. What he's calling you to, otherwise you might end up like Jonah in the belly of a whale, before you have to come to a realization that your task is where you need to be. So, it's very interesting to just to understand some of that background. And I suppose from my understanding and of reading of a lot of the things you have written, and I will let listeners know and readers know that there will be links to Michael's articles, there's half a dozen of them that were published on the Brownstone Institute website from about February this year and the interesting point to me, I suppose, is that Covid has been a wake-up call for us all, although many people didn't hear the call. And to me, it was a really significant change, that the world seemed normal, but really what was happening is that a lot of things were hidden that became made known at that time and. I'll just read a little bit from your article from February 3 that will give listeners an understanding. It says here in the article that Michael has written, *"from March the 30th, 2020 to March the 28th, 2021. The Australian Christian Church made a fortune from Covid Hysteria and laughed all the way to the bank along the way, the church conceived Covid Theology to cover the greed. How much do you need to buy a pulpit? The answer is not much about 500 bucks. While the church cowers to the state, the Bible talks a lot about freedom. Jesus once said so if the Son shall set you free, you will be free indeed. That seems unambiguous. That sums up Christianity. Most churches taught the opposite during martial law in Australia, March 2020 to April 2022. Priests, ministers, and pastors preached vaccine mandates, vaccine passports and loyalty to the state to keep people safe. The minority who refused to obey were condemned as fascists, enemies of God and worst of all, anti-vaxxers. Most churches sung from the same hymn: 'Follow the Science," and this is a serious problem for a faith that relies on the Supernatural."*

And just another quote: *"...why did the churches give up on God and embrace the state during Covid Hysteria? They didn't. They never left the state."*

I suppose your comments are certainly provocative. In

fact, I advised you to get someone else to start your car in the morning. But I think you've deliberately put out there the story which for me was the most significant story of my lifetime that somehow, I realized I suddenly saw the world in a completely different way. And I suddenly saw the church in a completely different way. Because, as you say, church leaders were promoting compliance with something that was clearly not true and you know the amount of it. I just think from first principles someone asked me yes yesterday. You know, when did I first become aware of the problem? And I said, well, you know, not long into the whole lockdown, I was trying to follow, I know a bit about epidemiology, and I know a bit about public health, and I was trying to work out. The story there was nothing that seemed consistent about the policies, and then the next thing there was Operation Warp speed and vaccines, which normally had a long period of investigation, were suddenly being rushed in production and people were being forced to take something that had no validity and was being backed up by a number of authorities of course, including the church, and even here locally. The local church shut down and you know it was a horrifying story really, when you look at it, but important because it demonstrated to me to me something that had been hidden away from us and that was the story of the power of the state, the way that we become, I suppose under state ruling increasingly so and then hidden from that really was the story of the church. So. Tell me about that whole period for you, because I think you started your Freedom Matters Today, in around September of 2021, so it was sort of 18 months into the sort of whole Covid story and you've been very productive during that time. And you've written extensively. So just tell me about your view of what this means for us because one of the reasons I'm talking to you today is that I think you've been a clear voice about what's happened both in society and in the church and what's staggered me is that people have just had the collective amnesia and have gone on as though nothing has happened, when in fact everything has changed as far as I can see. So. I'm sorry, that's a sort of a big group of things to throw at you, but just tell us a little about your realization about what was happening and then your decision to start Freedom Matters. Today on September 21.

Michael: Yeah. Well, thank you Reuben. That article really summed up I guess, and was a distillation of my thinking with Covid Hysteria up to that point and in particular there was massive corruption. It would be different if churches received no money from government, but they not only received millions of dollars in support in in funding subsidies at the same time, they were very quiet and also they promoted, many of them, promoted vaccines, vaccine passports and so on so there's an obvious, pro quid pro there and as to how many were actually people who were deliberately quiet because they've received the money, or whether this is a generalized criticism of the church, I think it is a job for researchers to go from church to church and work out whether their minister did or not, but I think generally speaking, churches, in every generation, Christians are challenged to stand for their faith. And so Covid Hysteria, I guess for me, Reuben, is the challenge of our generation or certainly one of them and Christians on the whole, failed appallingly. And there have been other crises in the past for different churches, different, I guess, issues, different ages, and different places. And often Christians get it right, and often Christians get it wrong.

Reuben: Can I just ask you some one point in that I was reading through, Michael's written a terrific book called *Freedom from Fascism* which I've got right in front of me here now and I finished it in the last week or so and I think it's really an important book and very important for people, whether they're Christians or not Christians, to read, because I think there's so much that you have in that area but one of the things that you haven't covered and I think it's significant is the complicity of the medical profession in this whole area and I suppose what was quite notable for me was early and I got into some discussion, and rigorous discussion with some cousins who were Christians, and they sent me something from the dentists and doctors, Christian Medical Association, or words to that effect and these guys were promoting the vaccine and the fact that really this is a gift from Jesus to a society. And I was just appalled at the whole story there. But I realized that we've got quite a complex system, because we've got, you know, the medical profession who have been really leaned on by the government and you know, it's no longer possible to get independent medical advice. We've got, you know, the legal system and emergency legislation and bio security legislation. We've got the story of what the government is doing. And then we've got, you know, major corporations as well. And so, we've been beaten in a pincer movement that trapped anyone that has an alternative. And also, we've been beaten because we're there's been a claim that this is the science, so it's been a very difficult story to find your way out of it, and because all the elements you know so many of my friends have gone to their local doctors who have really held the party line, even though when I interrogated many of the doctors, none of them had done any independent research, so it's been a terrible time for us as a society and I don't think we can just forget about it and go back to normal because, you know, there's no doubt what's coming will come again.

Michael: You're absolutely right. The churches behaved corruptly, absolutely and what happened with not only that, but they also created Covid Theology, which is the idea that you must submit to the state that Christians must obey the government, which means that every Anglican church in Sydney is sinning against God, every Anglican church, every Baptist Church, every Presbyterian Church, because The Protestant Reformation was a violent revolution against the Roman Catholic Church. It was not a pacifist movement. Hundreds of thousands of people were murdered and killed in wars and religious wars to break the power of Rome. In the Protestant Reformation, so there was Luther and Zwingli and others Calvin in Geneva and so on. But what it means is if the government must be obeyed at all costs, it means that every single Protestant is today continuing to sin against God, and they must return to the mother church. Then again, if we want to take it right back to the beginning, then the Roman Catholic Church sinned against the Orthodox Church for breaking away with them way back in the beginning as well. And then you have the American Revolution, which was a violent War against the rightful God ordained authority of Great Britain, and so this Covid Theology rubbish that the Anglican church, in particular Sydney and other places promoted, is completely straight from Hell. This is sort of demonic rubbish, it's complete and utter nonsense. Christians have a have a right to weigh and measure government policy, and civil disobedience was, in my view, the only option for

Christians as it was interestingly, with the civil rights movement in America. And I read recently that Billy Graham actually opposed the civil rights movement. He wouldn't participate in it because he believed that people must obey the government in everything.

Reuben: It's a challenging thing. If I can just intervene for a moment because I think the foundational verse really is the people of views is from the book of Romans, Romans 13, which says let every person be subject to the governing authorities for there's no authority except from God and those that exist have been instituted by God. So that's I suppose that's the foundational verse that people stand on. Well, I think that's the thing. But then it goes onto that Paul goes on to say a lot more. About that in relation to the 10 Commandments and so forth. But the issue, I suppose it's interesting is that people have used that, haven't they? And as you pointed out the church itself is on history, the Protestant Church is one of doing the exact opposite. Yeah. And your point is that the church in Australia and in the West, the same thing happened in the US who knows the billions of dollars that went to the church in various forms throughout the US, in money that flowed. But the church has been willing to take the money and therefore to not be critical of the government. So basically, I think in your book you say who he who pays the piper calls the tune and it's certainly true. And Michael, you've covered a much wider problem of the problem of the church and state. And I note that one of your great lines is *"don't follow the church, follow Jesus."* And that's such an important point because the church, I think, is lost to the structural Church and organized church has lost its way. And you know I've even been seeing that in terms of you mentioned the story of, you know, religious schools or schools, that of standing on Christian faith, that so many, you know, billions go to them from the state. And then I was thinking even in the theological colleges, they've all accepted state money in effect and come under state jurisdiction because you have to fall into line on under a particular umbrella to receive funding, so you know somehow, we've got ourselves into a terrible situation and I suppose not surprisingly then, when the government is organized, completely illegal process and invoked legislation, which has really been waiting there to trap us under emergency legislation, then the church has not said anything because its interests are to be aligned with the state and making money so it's a pretty terrible situation for us, isn't it?

Michael: It's an appalling situation. Effectively, what is proven is that Jesus came to build the Kingdom of God and he is, in a sense the one who ushers in the Kingdom of God and the church is interested in the Kingdom of the world. They're interested in their investments, their properties, their churches, their money. And particularly in the West, the Western churches have become so rich and so powerful that they believe they can change the minds of children, get them all good little future church attendees to bring in the money. And there's so much money, so much power. And this is desire to control the state, to control the government and control, but Jesus even when he was, before Pilate, he said *"My Kingdom is not of this world. If it was, my disciples would fight,"* and he came to die for the sins of the world he came to take all the sin of the world upon his own shoulders, and he by his death, he ended the power of the guilt and the and the penalty of sin for all who trust in Him and for me, that is the message of the good news and during Covid the churches should have continued to do that. They should have kept the churches open. They should have endured the cost, endured the fines, endured the persecution. But they didn't because they're gutless. They're basically grown fat and indolent and self-indulgent and corrupt basically. And if you look at the churches around the world who are Christian communities around the world that are suffering intense persecution, they don't have the beautiful churches, they don't have the schools, they don't have the investments, but they have true faith and this resilience. This remarkable faith that you don't see here.

Reuben: Its fascinating isn't it, Michael. It's fascinating to think that, as you say, that you know, some years ago, I remember I had a good friend that ended up in China. And it was very clear that because that's really what it comes down to. Despite a lot of persecution, the underground church in China was thriving and some estimated there were perhaps more than 100 million Christians. Even in Iran today, there are extraordinary numbers of people coming to faith under very, very difficult situations. So, what happens is that the church itself is indolent, as you say. And also, I suppose, because they're wealthy, they want to protect their assets rather than standing for truth. And it's quite an alarming situation to be in because I suppose what we are seeing is the church, the organized church is under judgement whether we realize it or not, and so it's a really important thing not to be working against God in this whole story. And I notice particularly, the word that that comes frequently in your writings is fascism. There's not any more general fascist behavior you talk about, but you also talk about Christian fascism. So, I think it's an important word to understand what you mean by it. And can you just elucidate on that? I came to quite a way through the book before I discovered some of the story about what you actually meant by fascism. So, it's quite an important term for us. So, can you just say a little bit more about what you understand by that and what you mean today?

Michael: OK. Yeah, that's great. Well, that was one of

the reasons I started Freedom Matters. Today, some people have said was it was a kind of criticism of Black Lives Matter, but, actually, I didn't even think about that until a few months ago. Freedom Matters Today is effectively freedom that Christ brings, and I made a list of freedoms. It was freedom from fascism and tyranny, freedom from fear and despair, freedom from guilt and sin, freedom from past and prejudice, and I think freedom from conflict and war, I think, was the last one and freedom from fascism and tyranny was the focus of last year's talks and books, freedom from fear and despair was the second theme and I was trying to think of what fascism meant because it was being bandied around by lots of people. It was called medical fascism, Covid fascism. The Left accused Donald Trump of being a fascist Donald Trump accused the others, but no one can really agree on a definition, so I came up with definitions of the political systems that we have, and I tried to think, OK, well, if you want to explain very simply to someone what is the difference between these different political systems, you have to come up with a very simple definition then. Communism is when power is vested in the state. So that's communism. The state runs everything. The state owns everything. Socialism is where everyone shares equal power in society, the concept of socialism, is equality, and everyone has equal share.

Reuben: Except as we know, some animals are more

equal than others.

Michael: Absolutely, absolutely. I'm just going with sort of the basic definitions. Democracy is where all people share power and elect someone to embody their will. So, everyone shares the power, they elect someone to embody the will of the people. So, the people in a sense, have the power. Fascism is where people voluntarily concede their power to a group of people or a person, and authoritarianism is when people are forced to concede their power to a group of people or persons. So, the difference between fascism and authoritarianism is that people in fascism voluntarily concede their power and we see that in every fascist society we see it in Spain, Portugal, Germany, Italy, Japan, they voluntarily conceded their power to a group of people or a person. And in every single case, fascism was born out of a dysfunctional democracy. So, democracy was decaying and dying. China can never be a fascist state because it's never been a democracy. It's an authoritarian state. Same with Russia. Russia can never be a fascist state because it doesn't come from democracy. So, for me, my understanding of fascism, in a secular sense, comes from my empirical observation that in every case democracy preceded as far as I know all the cases of fascism in the 20th century.

Reuben: In your book, you point out that democracy is only a relatively recent story, so we can't ignore a couple of thousands of years of history. The other, the supposed definition that's helped me. I'd like your view on it. Fascism involves a sort of emerging, not necessarily emerging better an interweaving of the of the state and industry, various industries that support the state and one of the things that's that seems to me helpful to understand the road we're going on is the rise of the private public partnership, which seems to be woven into everything even here in Australia. You know the, the way that some of the big accounting companies and advice companies have become into woven into government as being an example of a really dangerous situation of the of the state and their agreed supporters merging together in some sort of process that we don't even understand because it's often hidden behind the scenes for us. So yeah, it is one of the things you explain those were very helpful definitions. How would you see, I suppose Christian, Christian fascism, which you outline quite extensively in in your book?

Michael: It was, I think, simply put, Reuben, that fascism is where people voluntarily concede their power to a group of people or a person and so in the beginning of Christianity, everyone was given the Spirit, everyone was one in Christ, God taught them through his Holy Spirit. The role of the Spirit was and remains to be pointing people to the Son, teaching us about who he is, what he's done and why he's important and how we must follow him. And so, everyone was equal, equal but different if we'd like to use that term, people have different roles in the body of Christ. There was a very strong theme in Paul's writings. There was no church in the New Testament. There was only the body of Christ. There were gatherings and they became the church. The church, I guess, turned up later when it moved from a group of people to a place to an institution, and then it became hierarchy, priests appear on the scene, and they were the ones who had all the power or the authority. So, what happened was Christians voluntarily conceded their own authority God had given them to promote the Kingdom of God to others, and then once Constantine took over in 312 and was converted whenever it was, it became a nation state and so everyone was forced to become Christian. And so, it was the hierarchy, and then the interesting thing is as soon as they could they closed the Bible. And they prevented people from reading the scriptures for almost 1000 years. And the reason they did that is they didn't want people to know about God, yes.

Reuben: They wanted an interpretation by the authority that exists, which was then the church was the state. So that became quite significant. And I suppose you point out in your book, that you know, in terms of the roots of the Anglican church, the Church of England in England, that it's got a pretty sordid background, and led a waning of the church and the state and now it's I think it's quite damaging as far as you can see and the fact that the bishops sit in the House of Lords and so forth, there's all sorts of compromises that end up being made. And of course, that church is going downhill in numbers. And here in Australia, of course, is going downhill and in Western Europe. But the organized church and your focus, I think is so important because as we think of the church, we think of the organization, we think of the buildings, sometimes we think of the amazing cathedrals sort of throughout scattered throughout Europe. But your point is that the church is the called-out ones, the ones that have given their allegiance to Jesus and this is completely separate to the organization. In fact, organization is just by definition and can't help it become corrupt. There's no other way. Once you get man-made institutions that come into play so we're in a pretty serious problem here, because we're at the end of a couple of thousands of years of organizational failure that's had the gospel on what Jesus called people to.

Michael: Absolutely, it's interesting. But I don't have a problem with the government. A lot of people with Covid Hysteria have a problem with the government. I'm free to talk about these things. If I lived in a society run by the church, I'd be dead. They would have killed me a long time ago. It was, and that's what they do whenever someone in history has come up with the idea that the God speaks to us through his Word that we can open the Bible. We can pray, we can read it. We can make decisions based on what we've read. And we don't need to consult the priest or the pastor or the minister. And we don't need to be approved by the church or the hierarchy within the church, and people have been persecuted throughout history. That's what's happened throughout the centuries, whenever there's been a movement of people who have decided to, I guess follow where they think God has called them to go or to do, they have been persecuted. Even the idea of Christian mission work to China and India was met with severe opposition from the established church. So, we need to go back to the scriptures. And what I do with freedom Matters Today is I open the Scriptures and I look at a passage and think about what it means. I go back to the Greek and the Hebrew which I was trained with at Moore College and Morling College, and I try to explain what God is saying and what the text is saying to us as clearly and as precisely as I can and what I've discovered in my in my studies with freedom as I've looked at the Christ and the wilderness with the devil, the confrontation there, I've looked at Christian citizenship, I've looked at the role of the state, and so on and what I find is a rich reservoir of, I guess wonderful truth that, comes from the Bible to us, and I just encourage people to stop, I guess, offloading your faith to someone else take responsibility for the faith that God has given you and grow in your own faith each day by living out your faith in Word and deed, by practicing the love that God has given us. Jesus said he gave us a new commandment, which is to love others as I have loved you. And what did Jesus do? He laid down his life for his enemies. He loved his enemies. He laid down his life for his enemies. And so, as Christians, we don't have any enemy. And we are to love others by this sacrificial love. We are to walk alongside others. And in terms of the gathering, we don't need to go to. Church on Sunday. This phrase *'my family and I go to church,'* is actually an unbiblical statement. As I've said many times in the book, our identity is in Christ, our brothers and sisters are anyone who believes in Christ. Our identity is in Christ. Going to a church? How can you go to something if you are already part of that thing? And when you leave the church building, where is God then? And I talk about that in my book, what does God do during the week? And I remember asking my parishioners years ago, about that, that they couldn't understand. What's he doing? Is he hiding, waiting for us to come back?

Reuben: It's a bit like that. He is with us. I did like that little part where he said, *'what does God do during the week?'* as if he was sort of just away from the whole of his own creation, but what you point to Michael really is the story of the transformational work of God in the individual and I suppose the heart of the story is we can't try harder and have success. It's only God's transforming power by his

Spirit that can do it. Yes, and I think you draw us into a really important story and you I think you have been deliberately provocative in your book. And I'm sure that many in the church completely hate it because of that. But I think you've raised very important issues there. Just to conclude, I think you and I'd like to have another session with you, I suppose particularly relating to some of the events happening today and you've just been to Russia, which is a unique your location to go to. I didn't even know you could get go to Russia, but I'd love to talk to you about that. But I was thinking really about the, you know, one of the things that it doesn't talk about very much is the fact when I talk about judgement firstly, they don't talk because they don't talk really about Jesus coming again and you know what. Jesus points to a time when an evil leader will arise on the earth and people will be required to give their allegiance to him. And to me it was, I suppose, the Covid vaccine mandate and the Covid passport were just such a clear wake up call, but very few people heard that call because this is nothing less in a way than what is coming around that mark that the Bible tells us is going to be required to buy and sell. So, watch, I suppose the challenge is today for individual people of faith to stand for what is truth and against the overreach of both church and state. So, what do you think is the most effective way of facing the challenges to come?

Michael: Well, I think you're right. The church doesn't want Jesus to return, because that will mean the end of the gravy train and tax-exempt property investments. Most people go into the ministry today expecting a lift up in their salary and security. They can send their kids to good schools. We have really been weighed, measured, and found wanting in the West, it'd be interesting. I don't know. When I was in Russia, I did have a number of good conversations with some Orthodox priests. But one thing we didn't talk about would be the doctrine of the understanding of the coming return of Christ. It would be interesting to talk to those in the developing world about their understanding of the return of Christ. I suppose their belief must be more finely tuned than in the West. They don't expect him to return at all, but they focus on Moses and the law. But for us we are to run with perseverance, the race to the set before us, looking onto the author and finisher of our faith. That's Jesus. And we have a great cloud of witnesses and those. That cloud of witnesses Reuben, is not, you know, mum and Dad and Auntie Sue, but the great cloud of witnesses of the great Saints of the past, Abraham, Isaac, Jacob, and the prophets, the faithful who have followed Christ down through the centuries, the Old Testament Saints. They are a cloud of witnesses, and they are cheering us on, and they want us to look unto Jesus and to follow the Son, Jesus got baptized the Father said to the disciples of the baptism, *'This is my Son, whom I love, listen to him.'* And that is the call for Christians. Don't listen to the church or the pope or the bishop but open the scriptures. For English people, we're so blessed. There are dozens of translations. If you want to understand the Greek, there's a lot of material online that expounds the Greek text, word by word. But don't just read it, understand it and put it into practice. Go out and live your life. I was talking with a guy last night about Freedom Matters Today and he said *'Look, Michael, I don't agree with what you're saying but because it's you, I'll give it a go. It was just really encouraging because he said if it's from you, I'll give it a go. I'll read some material.'*

I thought we can make a difference in the lives of people around us and that is our world. Our world isn't the world of Trump or the lunatics in America with what's happening over there. Our world is here, amongst our families and friends, the people we know we are, in a sense, Christ in their presence, because we bring the words of Christ, the identity of Christ through what we say and what we do, we are, in a sense the Bible, or I guess, the witness of God to them. And that's really where we should be, be a light to the world, telling them about Jesus and living a life that we should live in full assurance and confidence before God.

Reuben: I like your focus, and it's really true, isn't it, that if you look at each of our own lives, most of us have been influenced by one other person that's had an impact and has brought the truth about who Jesus is into view for us. And that's been very significant. And as I look out across all the challenges we have, you know, one of the things that I realize is that we can only influence those that we have access to and also, we have to form communities where people can support and help one another in what's going to be ahead. It does seem as though what's meaning is going to be increasing government overreach. I know that you said you don't have a problem with government. I definitely do have a problem with government, and I can see I can see a vast overreach of government coming and it was evident through, so I suppose, we have to be prepared for trouble and it's really important. I think that your point is to somehow in the midst of all this madness, we have to take hold of who Jesus is and his word to see what he's calling us to which is to lay down our life for him and for others. And to love, he's called us to do the new commandment to love one another. And that's hard for us by our own effort, but quite definitely is a God who can transform us and transform our lives. So where do you see your next stage going from here in you've done extensive writings? I've enjoyed all the things you've written for the Brownstone Institute, and I've read just a couple of few books you've written. Also, some books of fiction. You've been very busy guy. Tell us about your plans for the future and where people can follow Freedom Matters Today?

Michael: Well, I've written a number of novels as you say I've written *The Curse of Crooked River,* which is a book I think a lot of readers from Australia might be interested in set in the gold rush period of the 1870s in Central West NSW. And it looks at a lot of the issues that we see in contemporary Australia, such as Aboriginal Australians and we're considering the process of the pastoralists and that history, and it is a it is a mystery. It's a great book. I wrote the, but it's been well received from by everyone I know who's read it. *The Third Tsunami* is set in Japan about a man who was a soldier who's coming to terms with that, and then he loses his family in the tsunami, and he encounters challenges as a Japanese man and how he fits into that world. Both the stories, interestingly, involve soldiers have come back from conflict and have to deal with what it means to live in a civilian world after being in the world of war, and it was sort of accidental in a way, but I think it really does speak to society today because we have so many soldiers who are fighting around the world and how do we deal with that and how do we adjust back to normal life after conflict. I've also written. *Monkey and the Castle by the Sea,* which is sort of philosophical book in one sense, is a good story about the ancient world before humans came along and the most controversial book, there was a bit of a pushback on *'Is*

Russia Our Enemy?' but I strongly believe that we don't wrestle against flesh and blood, but against principalities, powers and Christ defeated, diabolos in the wilderness. But he is diabolos and is still around. And he wants to destroy the testimony and I write about that.

Reuben: ...It's just sort of an extent of your writing. And I did enjoy, and I'll put in the this post your letter from Russia that you so it's one of things to be helpful to me is the great book. Because in that book it really highlights the story of somehow, we have to take a look that's 180 degrees away from the narrative being promoted by a range of increasingly small group of media barons and groups that are controlling the information so that we get. So, it's really important to really, you know, investigate what's behind this and not just accept the prevailing narrative. So, I'm really thankful for what you've done and particularly that you've been brave enough to go to Russia and be on the ground and check that out. So, I'd like to talk to you again about that. And it's been, it's been, it's been really wonderful to just have some time with you and talk about the central issue here, which is really faith, faith in God, the church and what it means and then what do we do in this response to something like government dramatic government overreach with, with Covid and the Covid lockdowns. And you've given us a lot of food for thought. And I'll point people to some of your brands. And you have your goals and your brave book Freedom from Fascism. It's clear that our interview must be coming to an end because my dog Snowy is out on the snow on the veranda barking, he thinks the time must be up. So, I'll have to go and let him in, in a moment. But Michael, thank you. People can follow you at, what is the web address for that?

Michael: freedommatterstoday.com. I have a weekly podcast now which people can listen to, and the question I'm asking until Christmas is who is Jesus?

Reuben: That's a great question. Well, look, I'll put that there. I got a link to your articles and to your books. I have enjoyed your writings very much and you know, whatever story is you're I think provoking those in the church and society to think carefully about what's going on and what their response. So, thanks so much for what you've done and the way that you provoked this. As I read the book, you provoke me into thinking much more attentive about what's behind this and some of the assumptions I've made.

Michael: Thank you very much, Ruben. It's been a great pleasure talking to you and God bless you with you in your book too. I read your book is a great book. It's a book for our time, ancient wisdom for modern times. I think it's a really good way of looking at and I wish you well with its success as well.

Reuben: Thanks, Michael. I appreciate it very much. And we'll look forward to talking to you again. I'm going to reflect on what we've been talking about, and you know the story of Russia is very much at the top of our mind today in so many ways because you can't help but think we're being drawn into a conflict which is not going to have a good outcome for anyone. And so, it would be good just to have some time to discuss that journey you've had. And it sounds like you're going to go there again. So that's wonderful. So, I'll talk to you again and we'll make another appointment to have another time together to form a podcast on my little podcast group here.

Michael: Thank you very much, Reuben. It's been wonderful.

Reuben: Thanks Michael. So, look, I hope you've enjoyed that interview with Dr. Sutton. I found the interview really interesting, and his books and articles are very worthwhile reading.

8

OCTOBER 7, 2023

Emeritus Professor Reuben Rose, Son's of Issachar Podcast, the Russia Ukraine Conflict, What's Next?' Podcast Episode

https://reubenrose.substack.com/p/the-ukraine-russia-conflict-whats

Topics: Ukraine, 2014 coup, American foreign policy, Fascism, Covid Hysteria, Russia.

TRANSCRIPT

Reuben: Dr. Michael Sutton. Following his recent visit to Russia, he spent 5 weeks in Russia and his evaluation is that the country is thriving. He's written an interesting article called *'Letter from the Forbidden Land,'* published recently by the Brownstone Institute. I've got a link to it in the newsletter. And here are a couple of more interesting quotes from the article: *"The West doesn't really care about the freedom of Ukraine as they are happily and blindly removing our freedoms from Washington to Canberra. We in the West face a relentless, persistent, and comprehensive assault on civil liberties, our freedoms, our beliefs, our faith, and our very existence from a virulent form of neo-fascism that has emerged like a cancer."*

Now about faltering democracy. In relation to future American betrayal, he says, *"It is my belief that at some point Ukraine will be betrayed by America. There are echoes of the Korean War, the Vietnam War, and the Spanish Civil War in this current malaise, and the ghosts and demons from those dark periods have been awoken from their slumber. If history is anything to go by, the West will not stand with Ukraine forever. And just like South Korea and South Vietnam, Ukraine will face the cold reality of American strategic realignment."*

In the next part of the article, he talks about Russians fighting for their homeland: *"The Russians are fighting for what they believe is their homeland, and this is what the West doesn't understand. In Donbass, they do not believe that this is anything other than Russian territory in fact, not a war against the Ukrainian people, but against American imperialism. When the most recent conflict began, most Ukrainians fled to Russia, than to the West. In fact, the largest community of Ukrainians in the world is in Russia. The Civil War in the eastern part of Ukraine has its roots in the US backed coup in 2014, when the democratically elected Ukrainian government was toppled and American moved there. There have been civil conflicts since 2014, and the death toll and psychological damage in the Donbass region has been catastrophic. But the western media made sure none of it made front page news for almost a decade. This is America's Ukraine, and Kiev knows it all too well."*

Now that's quite an extensive article written by Dr. Sutton which you can read with the link but here is the interview I did with Dr. Sutton did just a few days ago:

Reuben: So, Sons of Issachar listeners and readers, I'm very delighted to welcome back again, Dr. Michael Sutton, who is I worked out some sort of four P's. He's a priest, publisher, professor, let me think, what else. Yes, he's a podcaster. And what else would it be? Michael, you've got a range of strings to your bow, haven't you.

Michael: Political economist might be one.

Reuben: Of course, the most important part of your whole background, but I think when we talked last week about the challenges around Covid and how the church had responded in relation to some of your articles published in the Brownstone Institute, I noted that you'd written an article relatively recently, I think from Russia in August, in August this year and I thought it would be very useful because there's so much false information coming out and there's so many issues that we try to get to know, but we don't know because we don't have any firsthand information. It'll be great to have you speaking about your time in Russia, and as I was thinking about it, Michael, I noted that I detected it at the time and I think I saw it even in one of your books, that the war in Russia somehow cured Covid, so there's a link between Covid and the Russian Ukrainian war with the Russian invasion of Ukraine because all of a sudden I noted that in February, when this war started, Covid suddenly disappeared off the front pages. And then no one talked about it anymore, so just tell me a little bit about this because I thought that it was a remarkable event.

Michael: Well, thank you, Reuben. It's wonderful to be back on your podcast. Thank you very much for inviting me back again and thank you also for your warm introduction. As for Covid and Russia, the interesting thing about that relationship I wrote about in my first book, *Freedom from Fascism, A Christian Response to Mass Formation Psychosis* and that really was a talk about what was happening in Covid Hysteria was that many people have pointed out, not just me that it was a very concerted indoctrination brainwashing exercise, and we see proof of that by the fact that it in February 2022, when the conflict between Russia and America and Ukraine exacerbated, then suddenly as you say, Covid ceased to be of any importance. And so, this is often proof of some kind of indoctrination where suddenly something that was so vitally important to everyone's minds and hearts and conversations, suddenly evaporates and no one talks about it again, and it's completely removed from public discourse, and it's remarkable, in a sense that this is exactly what happened. So, I don't believe, there are a lot of people who talk about what is the 5G network and the phone network is sort of like amplifiers of indoctrination around the world. I think that if that was the case, if that was how people were indoctrinated, it would be incredibly easy for governments, they wouldn't have to do anything but turn on the switch and people would just go about their business, and you wouldn't need a large bureaucracy, just one person to turn off the switch but I do think what happens is that indoctrination is a much more sophisticated process.

Reuben: Just as an aside, you probably have read the book Laura Dodsworth's book 'State of Fear,' but that was a very powerful book for me because she looked at the intentional indoctrination by the UK government. They even formed a committee of all the psychologists which included a well-known communist psychologist on that committee to really change the whole approach in Great Britain about the whole story with Covid and vaccinations. So, it was very clear cut, and you know, there was a real intentionality behind it, we've guessed from other points of view and in other countries, but it was very clear that the indoctrination process has been become very sophisticated and very clever, hasn't it.

Michael: Absolutely, and governments do it all the time, as I said in *Freedom from Fascism*, governments engage in propaganda all the time. Sometimes they do it to hurt us. Sometimes they do it to help us. Sometimes it is with pernicious intent. Sometimes they really don't know what they're doing and it's to cover up mistakes, and so on, and they have been working on these exercises for decades, and in World War 2 of course, there were, there was intense propaganda effort to promote loyalty within the state for the state to support war against Germany and Japan, and then it took us probably until the 50s when that sort of psychosis or that war mentality could be stripped back, and that was a very intense program, but in this particular time, what's interesting is that as soon as the conflict began, a number of lies began to sort of permeate the discourse and the narrative, and one of the lies is that the war began in February 2022. That's not true. There's been conflict with the republics that declared independence from 2014 when they broke away from Ukraine and they declared independence and autonomy, there's been violent conflict, civil war, words used by the Lowy Institute. So, the lie is that the war began in February 2022, and you see this again, it's like with Covid, there are certain statistics, this is day 550 day 556, pretty much like that Satanic Mass episodes we had with Covid where the former Premier, thank God is gone, she would stand on TV and talk about the death toll and it was sort of like a Satanic Mass, it was to remind people this crisis was ongoing so that's the first lie. The second lie was that it was unprovoked aggression, it was an unprovoked aggression. These conflicts began with the toppling of that democratically elected regime in 2014, the breakaway of the two of the of the republics, the Donetsk and Luhansk and then of course, the Russians accession of Crimea. So this is a long term, complex, complicated conflict, and the media does, and what they did in Covid and what they did with Trump is that they take something very complex and very complicated and very much rooted in many variables and then make it very simple, there are good guys and bad guys and I feel like Reuben, if you have kids going through school, it's like the teacher says, *'listen, boys and girls, I want to tell you about goodies and baddies and the baddies, they're Russians and they are all evil and the goodies, well, they're Americans, and please remember this,'* and this is the level of stupidity, and idiocy, taking something so profound and complex, and so, for example, another complexity is that when in February 2022, when this conflict took off, more Ukrainians fled to Russia than to the West.

Reuben: Actually, just to see that in your article and that's, you know, it's one of those things that isn't known, as you said, there's a very simple story being put above but it is interesting, Michael, listen, as you look back to the Obama administration and the role that Joe Biden played and was affected in that vital period around 2014-15 was in Ukraine a lot, it was when Hunter Biden was being paid a lot of money for we don't know what and the interesting thing about it is, is that almost as soon as the Trump campaign started, in the 2016 election there was a sort of a desire to tar him with a brush to Russia, being pro-Russian and yet really the issues of Ukraine lurked in the background all the time. There were these huge amounts of money, but we don't still know where all those sources of money go, but it's certainly interesting from my reading, at least to see that the period around 2014 was critical because there seemed to be a CIA involvement, a stimulation of an uprising, and then a range of things fell out of that and it seemed to be a provocation of Russia that's continued so it's really hard to get a handle on it all, but I suppose if we could follow the money trail, we'd have a better understanding.

Michael: Yeah, I think the reality is that for some

bizarre reason, Joe Biden's family and corporation, is knee deep in the Ukraine and there's so much information about that out there, but no one's allowed to talk about it, which is interesting in itself, so, for some reason, Joe and Ukraine are intimately tied together and so history is screaming out for the truth, and the truth is out there, but we're not allowed to talk about it, and that's interesting in itself, but also the other thing is Reuben, that what I find curious about this whole process particularly for a lot of people who are concerned about the role of America and so on it's not unusual behavior for America, in terms of its control of the world, and it's desire to pursue its national interests. So, in the Cold War, the enemy was the Soviet Union and China or anything that resembled communism, even Australia was scrutinized under the good old days of Gough Whitlam, they were very concerned about Gough and some of his policies, rightly so I suppose in hindsight, but they actively toppled the Allende regime in Chile in 1973, in a way similar to what really happened in Ukraine. But they were promoting their national interest, their priority was to was eradicate communism and all forms of communism around the world, and Allende was a socialist and even though he was democratically elected, they just didn't like him and they wanted to get him out and they put the fascist Pinochet in charge, and he went around killing people until he eventually left and so America is sort of behaving the way it's always behaved. It promotes its national interest, as all countries do and for Ukraine, Ukraine is a nation of vast economic resources, mineral deposits and so on, and so is Russia. Russia is an enormous country in terms of mineral resources. That a country like America would desperately need in the time of decline and America is declining and so if they can get into Russia, if they can get access to those vast mineral deposits, resources to promote their economy and economic development, they will do it, yes. And so that's the long game that they're playing. They want Russia and the resources there and so the goal is that.

Reuben: Obviously, the Ukrainian resources, could see a lot of involvement of groups like Black Rock and others to look at privatizing various things and taking over the Ukrainian economy at the time that the war has ended, so it's very clear that there's a deal being done and there's a there's a vast economy to take control of if they can get it.

Michael: That's right. Well, they want to do to the Ukraine what Yeltsin did to the Russian economy, which was to privatize it under the so-called principle of free trade. But he gave entire industries to his friends, yes, and created a system of oligarchy capitalism that continues to puzzle a little because it is a capitalist system. It is a market-based society, but it is one where there are very powerful people who were given positions of incredible economic strength simply because they knew Yeltsin. And so, what's gonna happen in Ukraine is basically the same thing, except it will be done under the cover of democracy and freedom. And the people who will lose out will be the Ukrainian people who will suddenly realize *'We don't own anything. None of our sectors are owned by Ukrainians.'* It will all be owned by Americans and the Europeans and the British and the Australians will be in there. So, it's what you will see that is affecting an entire society.

Reuben: Thanks for the great story that the World Economic Forum has for while that in 2030 we will own nothing and will be happy. But it looks like they'll be happier. Tell me this, I suppose the interesting thing to me that you even try to go to Russia at this time, I didn't even know you're going get there. So, tell us a bit about your trip and how, how you came to go and how you overcame the various barriers to actually get there.

Michael: We're not allowed to go to Russia from Australia, the DFAT website says. Russia is a no-go area, it's on the verge of collapse apparently, there's threats of terrorism across Russia, which is interesting and travel insurance is not available from this side, and there's also no currency exchange. You can't exchange money which is discrimination against all the Russian Australians who live here and their family in Russia and lots of people. Interestingly, just before I visited Russia, there was an enormous economic affairs event at St Petersburg promoting economic development and promoting international affairs there was an enormous delegation from American business, promoting American trade. So how did they get there and how did they get travel insurance? It's a historical thing that whenever governments impose a barrier, private organizations or quasi-government organizations will find a way around it and so that's what they've done, sanctions are a very ineffective instrument to make it appear that the government is doing something or make it appear that government looks like it's doing something, where in fact it is not doing anything, and so what, what the situation is I've never seen so much food in my life. When I went to the supermarkets there was an abundance of resources, fresh fish, caviar, wine, and I was going around and seeing all the companies that were not supposed to be there and making a list of all these companies. *'What are you guys doing? You made a statement in Australia that you wouldn't have anything to do with Russia and how is it I can buy your products from the local shelf?'* And what was interesting is some of the really big companies, big corporations are still operating in Russia. I'm not gonna name them, I don't think it's appropriate to name them who's in, who's out, but it's interesting McDonald's decided to sell up and they sold it to a Russian entrepreneur, and he immediately saw this as a wonderful opportunity to appropriate technology that another country had protected for, you know, 50 years or whatever it's been. And they converted it into an even more popular restaurant called I think it's called in English, *'Yummy. That's it.'* And people go to *'Yummy, that's it,'* and every time you see a 'Yummy that's it,' restaurant in Russia, it's like a McDonald's here, there's cars lined up and the place is packed. And for the first time in a McDonald's-style restaurant, I ate hamburger that was edible. It was edible. I thought, wow, it actually tastes like real food. What have they done? Maybe we need more of *'Yummy, that's it,'* around the world.

Reuben: That's a remarkable thing isn't it, that sanctions can be a way of strengthening a country because it makes the country itself fall back on its own resources. And so, it's fascinating to see that that you know the economy actually seems to have been strengthened. I suppose Russia is now trading in rubles and gold as well. And you know, I don't know all the outcomes of the South African meeting with the BRICS group, but there's clearly been deals done with the BRICS countries and Russia seems to be thriving. Were you yourself having any problems in exchanging money for rubles and what money were you able to use?

Michael: No, no problems at all, you simply go to a Russian bank and they only accept American dollars or European Euro and they do Australian dollars, some of the banks, but I got my money converted into American dollars and then went to exchange in Russia over there so there was just a hiccup, I suppose but there were no barriers to travel. In fact, it made it easier to go to museums and to enjoy tourism in Russia. But what it has done, and I think a lot of Australians don't understand about Russia, and one of the things is interesting is in Australia, almost every single thing you buy is made in China, Australia makes virtually nothing today. But in Russia, it's the opposite. There are many, many things that we would buy from China that are Russian made and this has always been the case in Russia. What this conflict has done, it's turned Russians into themselves as opposed to promote themselves or to develop new entrepreneurial skills to build things that they wouldn't otherwise have done through globalization and so what this conflict has done has actually, it is making Russia great again. And so, it's doing to Russia what Trump desperately wanted to do for America, he wanted to make America great again by kicking out the foreigners. So, what they've done is actually kicked the foreigners out of Russia and made Russia great again. And so that's the great irony of this conflict. We don't have a history of massive economic development in Australia, we don't have the industrial capacity. We've never had, maybe in between the 1870s, probably to the 1950s there was the possibility that Australia could become an industrial superpower, but we were deindustrialized by the British and deindustrialized by America under this free trade nonsense, but it was incredible to go to some of these old factories, they've been building things, steel products for hundreds of years and this is incredible stuff, you know, you just see these enormous wheels and enormous machinery and tractors and engines, and all the things that go into making steel products and they've been doing this for hundreds of years and they continued through communism. They just changed the name on the front of the entrance to the building, continue to make it for the state. And today they're doing the same thing. And it's incredible, actually. When you think of Russia you think of drab skies, Red Square, but Russia is a remarkably productive, industrious country and their factories are incredibly extensive, beyond anything I've ever seen even in the United States.

Reuben: Goodness, Michael, where did you fly into Moscow? How long were you there and what was your itinerary?

Michael: I was there for about five weeks and flew into Moscow. Moscow was a very quiet place. We went, I went to Red Square. Beautiful place. One thing that really struck me with Russia is that they have a very keen sense of history, very keen sense of their war against fascism, what they call the Great Patriotic War. We're not allowed to talk about that these days. We talk about World War 2, and we like to emphasize you know, it was only Hitler and a few of his friends who were baddies. The rest were really good people. But history has a different story. Over 30 million Russians were killed by the Nazis. And so everywhere you go, there are these monuments to the war, to the victims of conflict. There are in every town and every village, anti-fascist statues and memorials. Every single person in Russia had someone in their family killed by the Nazis. So, they have a very strong sense of their past. I even saw a Nazi War Memorial War cemetery where the Nazis who fought against Russia were buried with respect and their German descendants can go to these specially designated, I suppose cemeteries and visit their loved ones which I thought was a very interesting reflection.

Reuben: And that's interesting, Michael isn't it, because one of the things I noted about Putin's speech, back around the time the conflict started was his reference to the Nazis in Ukraine and it's hard for us to understand. We thought it was just a beat-up. But I think it was a genuine issue as we know with a lot of the Azov battalion, but what you're alluding to is the fact that the story of the Nazis and their impact is still uppermost in mind for the Russians, because of the horrific story of what happened during the Great Patriotic War and the numbers of people who were killed.

Michael: Yeah, the war against fascism has never ended, and what we've seen, one of the things we have seen as a result of this conflict is the revival of fascist traditions in Eastern Europe from Finland to the Ukraine, Latvia, places like that, we see a push against the West in Slovakia with the new Prime Minister, the new leader of that country, where he is becoming more pro-Russian. But there are a lot of fascists. These are not Neo fascists, they're not the, you know, the skinheads running around Sydney with their black shirts and their sneakers, but these are the old fascists, the ones who loved Hitler, who adored Hitler, who love the good old days, who fought against Russia, fought against the West. In Latvia, there's the Latvian legion. In Ukraine, there's the Azov Battalion, there are lot of neo-Nazi, a lot of Nazi groups fighting for Ukraine. We had that in the Canadian Parliament, the guy who was applauded. He was a Nazi. The Polish wanted him extradited for war crimes, but we're not allowed to talk about it. This is a taboo subject and unfortunately what happened during the Cold War is that a lot of the fascists were rehabilitated, they were brought into America and into Russia for the Cold War scientific programs brought into NASA, and so on thousands of Nazi ended up in Australia, thousands of them went, you know, to the United States and the Nazi spirit is still alive and well. This underlying hatred for Israel, yes, this despising of Jews, we see it in Australia. I was even talking to someone the other day and they brought out all the old cliches and all the old anti-Semitic stuff and I was astonished when I heard it and they said, *'well, you know the Jews had it coming.'* And I said, *'well, I don't believe that at all, I think that's a terrible thing to say,'* and their response was *'well, you know what they're like.'* So, my response was, *'OK, well, tell me, what are they like?'* He said, *'You know, they all stick together.'* And I said, *'well, so do the Italians and the Greeks. Have you ever met Italians who don't? Family is the most important thing for them, so they stick together. What's the other slur against the Jews?'* He said, *'well, you know the problem with the Jews is that they're really successful,'* but isn't that what we're supposed to be in Australia? Isn't that what we promote in Australia, success? He had this terrible anti-Semitism, and he was a German Australian, German, of German descent, and his parents taught him that the Nazis were justified in exterminating the Jews, and it's unacceptable. And so, the war against fascism continues and so if you want anyone to get rid of Nazis, Russia's the one to do it because they hate fascism more than they hate anything.

Reuben: Yes, and Michael you must have talked to a lot of ordinary people around in the five weeks you were there, what's your sense of it, is there a common view about the war and what's happening with Russia and how they see things developing? And how they see President Putin.

Michael: Well, I think the other thing people don't

understand about Russians is that Russians are people who love their country as Americans are people who love their country. Russians love, love their nation, and what they see is the West trying to destroy Russia and they see this and they can't understand why the West hates Russia and the why the West wants to destroy Russia because they saw with the Cold War, the end of the Cold War they honestly believe that there was going to be some kind of détente, some kind of reconciliation with the West that it was kind of an acceptance of Russia and acceptance of America. But what they've realized is that the West is out to get them. The West wants to take over Russia. So Russian people are patriotic people. They love their country and there's nothing wrong with loving your country. Australians are taught to love their country. Americans love their country, and they are very nationalistic people. But you know, they're like everyone else, they want a happy life, they want a good job, they want happy family lives, they want to get on with life and what amazes me when I was in Russia, ordinary people are getting on with their lives, they have careers, they're seeking opportunities and I think what's happened since Yeltsin departed is the revitalization of the Russian economy in the long term so Russia went through a very tumultuous people in the 90's the collapse of the Soviet Union, but it's been gradually coming out of that that dark period to the point where you travel around Russia and you see apartment complexes in new suburbs, new economic development, new roads, industrial expansion. And there's you know, there's the reality of Russia is the same elsewhere if it will be in a capitalist society, there's disparity of income, there are poor places, there's wealthy places that we have that here. If you go out to Country NSW, you'll see poor towns, wealthy towns and so on. It's a reflection of the normal processes of economic development, and that's what really surprised me about Russia. It goes against what we've been taught about Russia. I was astounded at the economic development and the Russians only have three months out of the year to do anything because it's too cold to do anything. It's impossible to build during winter, so during summer they're doing everything that needs to be built or made or repaired or renovated. That's done within four months of the year. And when we were there, we saw all this activity with the Russian people, they were industrious and entrepreneurial and from a from a business point of view and I saw a lot of things. I was invited in to see some great success stories in one corporation there in Russia and it was called Sima Land, it's an industrial company, a little bit like Russia's Amazon, incredible business. And what they were doing was they their wholesale business and so on and we were shown all these enormous office spaces with thousands of employees, all in front of their computers, sending products all around Russia all around the world, and then then one of the rooms we saw up on the board there were that was a hundreds and hundreds of computers, all these technical things that they, you know, corporations have these days, and there was a big screen and CNN was being broadcast. So, they're watching CNN, so it's not a country where you're not allowed to watch the news, you're not being controlled, and I thought that was interesting. And then at the end of every morning at this corporation which had 14,000 employees, they're all young people between their early 20s. If they work in this company for a few years, they get enough money to put a deposit down for a house or an apartment so it's enabling a new generation to rise up, to have jobs and to improve themselves. And these are all positive things. And so, a lot of people, particularly young people, are investing in the future of Russia. I didn't see any evidence of people fleeing Russia and rushing to the West because they're Russian people, they love their country, they want to improve their country and then the most astounding thing at the end of the day was the end of this morning session was they played the national anthem of Russia. And I was, I was moved by it, I was really moved by it because I looked around at all these employees and they're all singing the national anthem of Russia. And once the anthem was over, I thought, well, America's had it.

Reuben: That's very interesting, isn't it? Last week there were drills around possible nuclear conflict and various parts of Russia and. The people, I mean, is there a sense of concern about the future and the conflict with the West, or how do people see that conflict and what do you think is the likely end point of this whole story that we're seeing?

Michael: Lots of great questions there, Reuben, it's difficult to know, really, I think that Russia is a vast country and I think that's another thing that we need to see is Russia's a little bit like Australia and it's like asking someone from Perth, what do you think's happening in Sydney and how does it impact? And someone will, from Perth will say well it's not really part of my world in the sense I don't see it. It's not part of my life and Russia's a little bit like that. They say that it's midnight in one part of Russia and its midday at the other part it's such a large country. And such an ethnically diverse country. And there's lots of local issues. There's lots of every regions and each is governed by a regional governor. There's the Parliament of the Duma, every regional group has its own parliament. They get elected like, like in a democracy. There's also the National Duma as well. There are many levels of bureaucracy, much like Australia and every region, is responsible for, I guess the infrastructure of that region, much like Australia is, so NSW was responsible for roads and so on and it's the same in Russia. So, Russia has all these different regional groupings. And what's interesting about that is that there is a sense of identity within Russia, not only for the nation but for the local area, and that is a really important thing, and so, we see in the conflict in Ukraine, those two areas in the Donbass region, the Donetsk and Lugansk regions, they are regional groups where there is a strong local identity of who they are as a people in the same way that Russia is an enormous country, but there's also strong regional identity, not so much in Australia. We play it out in football games, but we don't really have a strong New South Welshman or Victorian identity, but in Russia, there's a strong sense of local identity. And so, for these people in those autonomous republics are the ones who wanted the autonomy. They have a strong regional identity and many of them are Ukrainians who speak Russian many of. them are Russians who speak Ukrainian, Russians who speak Russians, Ukrainians, who speak Ukrainian and they're in these regions. They have this strong identity, and they want to be free. They want autonomy and ironically, that's what the West promoted for everyone else. They said you guys can be free and we will support freedom. Then these two independent regions, these two republics, they say we wanna be free but then, no, you're not allowed to be free you have to be part of the Ukraine. And so, there's that. And I think for me what we've seen since 9/11 is that the world watches and America behaves much the way all countries do, but they look at America and they think, well, what you say is not what you believe. And what we see is China trying to look at America during the War of terror and realized that America basically is a hypocritical liar they are promoting freedom and they go and turn, you know, they turn the Middle East back to the Stone Age and they engage in war for 20 years and despite promoting this idea, we believe in peace with democracy, freedom and all that, China observed America's wars and though well everything America says needs to be reevaluated and so America did itself terrible harm through the War on Terror. And now with this promotion of conflict in Russia and so America is its own worst enemy in a sense. And so, Russia and China and other countries, they're looking at America, they study America, you know, like how Magpies, they'll get you as you're walking along, they just observe you and think *'You're too close to the nest. Maybe I'll bomb you and rip out your eyes today.'* And that's what these countries are doing. They're looking at the United States and what they see is this profound dissonance between what America says and what America does. And I think there was a time, probably from Nixon up until Clinton, where Nixon and Clinton both shared the belief, and so did Kissinger, the belief that there could be a world of cooperation there could be coexistence between these superpowers, and then suddenly that changed. And so,

Russia and China are reevaluating their relationship with the West, and they just don't trust America and Britain, they don't trust them because everything they say turns out to be a lie.

Reuben: No, it's very difficult. Is that because you know, while America had, I suppose a succession of leaders who promoted freedom. What they've done is to undermine some of the aspects of freedom and so it makes it very difficult for people then to trust what they're doing and with the Biden administration and the ongoing conflicts, the story of the Middle East has been horrific in the amount of money they've spent over there, but now we've got this interminable conflict with the Russians and the Russians assumption is a long term view, a bit like the Vietcong in Vietnam, you know that these guys are gonna take a much longer term view than the West is able to sustain in terms of the amount of money and supplies that need to go on in the long term. Do you see this petering out or do you think there's going to be a momentous event, or you know what's happened so far, it seems, is what you're saying is that the sanctions, etc. that have been imposed have actually strengthened Russia. But you know, I suppose everyone's thinking to themselves what's going to happen and are we going to be drawn into a more extensive conflict because now, you know, there's hints of the UK sending more soldiers or so-called advisers into Ukraine, and you know there's quite a risk of the West getting drawn in deeper into this conflict.

Michael: Yeah, well, it looks like the new Vietnam now all over again. We were lied to in the 70s and 60s about what was happening in Vietnam. So, it looks like a new Vietnam. Almost every weapon, Reuben, that's been invented in the last 30 years, has been tested in Ukraine, now they've used every weapon that they could ever get their hands on, the people who suffer are the Ukrainian people. The answer, of course, is for both parties, all parties, America, of course, and their puppets in the Ukraine or their democratically elected leaders of course, and Russia of course to sit down and negotiate the autonomous regions to give autonomy to those regions and to allow peace to reign effectively allow those reasons to be autonomous and to be free, which is what they want. And it is consistent with the promises that it has elevated for the last 30 years, which was that any country or any group of countries that want to be free should be allowed self-determination. Isn't that what we're voting for with the Voice? Isn't that what we're voting for with the voice? And so we have in Australia, we have the people saying, well, Aboriginal people, they need a Voice they need self-determination effectively to organize their affairs well. Maybe it's interesting to see the same people promoting the Voice are the same people say well, those autonomous regions are not allowed to have independence. Why? And then they're the same people who are saying that Irian Jaya, should be free from Indonesia. OK. So, Irian Jaya can be free, the aboriginal people can be free, but the republics in eastern Ukraine cannot be free because America won't let them be free and so there's a strange inconsistency and hypocrisy and the ideology that has been promoted. And so, the world watches and the world realizes the inconsistencies and hypocrisies. In 2019 there was a factory in Russia, that was turning out 1,500 battle tanks and Russian battle takes a pretty impressive and that was before the conflict really exacerbated; 1,500 battle tanks from one factory. And there are hundreds of these factories from all over Russia all over Russia, so Russia will prevail in this conflict, is likely to prevail the people who will suffer, of course will be the Ukrainians, most of whom are poor, most of the rich Ukrainians left came to Australia and many of them are doing quite well here. Australia has thrown hundreds of millions of dollars to the Ukrainian community. They're in a sense queue jumping. And remember that too they get special treatment in Australia for some reason at the expense of all the other ethnic groups who have also legitimate claims of refugee status, but they're ignored because they're not white people, and so they're getting a lot of, money, a lot of support. A lot of benefits for the Ukrainian community, how the men were able to get here it's just another interesting question since the government in Ukraine expects them to fight for their country but the other thing is of course is that the people in Ukraine, the ones who are there are poor people because they could not afford the plane trip to Australia or America and they are the ones who suffer, at the end of the day, we simply have to stop arming the Ukraine so they can fight Russia. If they want, let them fight Russia, but by arming Ukraine with billions of dollars for weapons, we are just simply prolonging the conflict that will have the same outcome. And the other question is where is the United Nations, yes, under the United Nations I thought, you know the way to deal with these conflicts was to send the peacekeepers in. What happened to that and there's no United Nations, there's no end in sight because the American government desperately wants Biden to get reelected next year, they certainly don't want Trump reelected. And my take on the whole thing is it could either go two ways, it could be this long-term conflict of the 20 years like Vietnam, or it could be over the next year when Biden gets elected and he will negotiate a special treaty with Russia, and he'll get the Nobel Peace Prize for bringing peace to the world.

Reuben: I don't think Biden could negotiate anything, so it would certainly have to be his advisers that run everything in the background but it's an interesting thing that the war is totally being sustained by foreign dollars and the US and UK prepared to fight to the last drop of Ukrainian blood, and so it's a shocking situation that we find ourselves in and being part of and it's good to have some clearer viewpoint, Michael from you so it's very, very helpful and I suppose, just the final the situation is that part of the aim it seems of the West was to see Putin go. And yet I suppose for you know, 28 years he's been at the helm. And has overseen a dramatic improvement in the whole of the of the Russian economy and so. It could be an unstable period in Russia couldn't it because there's a range of obviously interests there. And Putin's health is rumored to be poor. What do you think? What is going to happen, or do you think that the extensive nature of Russia and the various regions will prosper in the long term no matter who is at the helm.

Michael: I think as Christians, what we have to do is embrace the refugees who have come, Ukrainians, whether they are rich or poor, we need to love them and embrace them and bear their burdens, many of them are pro-Russian ones as well and we need to bear their burdens in the years ahead because in a conflict zone of men will come home because Australia is their new home, and they'll have so many mental problems from the war and we need to walk with them and we can in terms of promoting peace Christians should promote peace because Jesus said blessed are the peacemakers. And churches don't talk about that, they support war. Blessed be the peacemakers so Christians should be more on the side of the peace promoting peace. If the Western church thinks that the Russians will rise up against their leader to institute democracy, that will involve sin right, Romans 13, so if we are to submit to our government, then Russians must submit to their government because, according to all religious traditions and the church, leaders are ordained by God. And so that means Vladimir Putin is ordained by God, and if we have a problem with that we need to revisit the essential doctrines of the Bible because if Anthony Albanese was ordained by God, then so was Valdimir Putin, and so we need to be very careful about telling other people to do something we need to do ourselves, and that's what the Bible calls hypocrisy.

Reuben: Yes, so it I means I suppose what you're saying is that we need to be on the side of peace in a world dominated by conflict in many ways. There are many evil actors working behind the scenes in the areas of conflict, because I suppose there's so much money to be made and it's a really critical time in the world because you can see that there are various forces that are trying to drag us into a complete, you know, a complete conflict. And in fact, trying to push us into a nuclear conflict. So, it's very interesting just to hear your perspective from your time in Russia and particularly I suppose, as just to hear, apart from anything else, how Russia, Russia is prospering as sanctions have been applied that people have had to be more industrious,…We like to think of Russia as one country but there are seven time zones, we need to think of several communities with their own backgrounds and their own history, and obviously to hear of your own experience there, it was a very positive experience and I think you mentioned that you might be going back there in the not too distant future.

Michael: It is definitely a country I would like to visit again. It's like a hidden civilization, it's like a hidden civilization from one of the comic books you read as a kid, and it is so incredible and so amazing. There's so much culture there, so many museums to visit, there's almost no one there. There was a Monet, Van Gogh and a couple of Picasso and all in one room. And I went to another room, it was full of Picasso. And it was just this culturally rich experience that was incredible, and you could fly to Russia. Simply go to museums for a week and then fly home.

Reuben: Where did you fly from?

Michael: Sydney. There are only a few airlines to get there you know, which is really stupid for me. You think the companies would want to take advantage of the opportunities that present themselves. What it is again, is a loyalty test. We have to be loyal to the state and the state has told us that we must *'Stand with Ukraine'* and when this nightmare is over then we will be told what to believe next and the church will sign up to the next one which will probably be climate change, and you will watch all the churches sign up to climate change and you will yes we will support climate change, and the next one will be China war and you will watch all the churches sign up to war with China, because they will do as they are told, unfortunately, what these conflict tells me is that the new Covid is this conflict with Russia. The new Covid is the conflict with Russia and there is all this discussion and focus now on Trump – who cares about Trump, and talking about the World Economic Forum, whereas talking about Russia as the new Covid Hysteria and everyone is as blind as they were during Covid Hysteria because, there is this constant *'Stand with Ukraine,'* but what does this mean, and most people don't even know where the Ukraine is. So, I encourage people to get out and meet Russians and befriend Russians and Ukrainians and in Australia develop relationships with them. Befriend them, learn about their culture and their history because they come from a remarkable part of the world that preserved Christianity for centuries and was a great defender of the Christian faith for centuries against the power of Islam and without that bulwark against Islam and against Hitler, we would all be Nazis now.

Reuben: That's a great thing to remember. There's a

great line. Without Russia, we would all be Nazi. It's been great and it's been great to talk to you just to get a little bit more insight into Russia from firsthand experience, and surprisingly just the way the country seems to be prospering economically at the moment. And you know as you say, the only consolation is for this war to come to an end somehow, and the simplest way is just to cut off the funds, supplies, funds that are coming to the Ukraine. But it's very hard to see. There are so many vested interests here at work. It's going to be hard to see this happening in the foreseeable future. We just hope it doesn't escalate further. But your viewpoint today has been very helpful for listeners to really understand a little bit more about what's happening from a person that's been there and experienced the country firsthand. And Michael, I do appreciate taking his time today very much.

Michael: Oh, thank you very much, Reuben. It's been a great pleasure and great experience, and I would be happy to come on your podcast again anytime, and it's been a great, great conversation. I just want to tell your listeners that there are many Australian Russians and there are many Australian Ukrainians and they're feeling a lot of tension, a lot of pressure at this time, and I think they need a lot of prayer, particularly Russian, Australian kids, and Ukrainian kids. There's a lot of, there's a lot of suffering in these communities and a lot of this is persecution of Russian people because of the conflict and it's unjustified, it's unacceptable and we need to keep the kids in mind, we need to pray for the communities, and we need to pray for governments here making these decisions that they make decisions that are consistent with what God wants.

Reuben: I think something that's really good endpoint and thanks very much for your time and I look forward to welcoming you back in the not-too-distant future because there's many other issues to discuss. And as you're hinting at the issue of the climate hysteria is going to make its way into the forefront of everything in the future, and so we might have a discussion about that sometime, but it's always good being able to discuss this subject where neither of us have got any expertise at all, and I think the world the world belongs to, those who know nothing and try to answer this so thank you for your time, it's been great. Thank you.

9

27 OCTOBER 2023

Interview with Hrvoje Moric, on the "Hrvoje Moric Show," TNT Radio,

https://tntradiolive.podbean.com/e/michael-sutton-on-the-hrvoje-moric-show-27-october-2023/

Topics: Israel, Baby Race, Forgiveness, Revenge, demographic change in the West

TRANSCRIPT

Hrvoje: Returning to the rebel transmission we have the Reverend Doctor Michael J Sutton, political economist, Professor, priest, pastor, now publisher, CEO of Freedom

Matters, today looking at freedom from a Christian perspective. I think one of the last times we chatted, he was out there in Russia. He has since returned. The website is Freedom Matters Today. I just saw on the website, I think he's got a new book just published 10 days ago, Baby Race. How's it going, Michael?

Michael: Hi Hrvoje, I'm well, it's always really wonderful to be with you again. I hope you're doing well. Thank you for inviting me back on and yes, Baby Race has been published recently. It's looking at demographic change in developed countries, it's the discussion over the debate of low fertility and whether nations should encourage families to have more kids and the common argument in the West is that we need to have more children, otherwise the social and economic fabric of the nation will collapse. I present a critique of this, and I look at 500 years of economic thought and look at various perspectives and I look at America, Japan, all of East Asia, and the population policies of particularly in East Asia in the 50s, 60s and 70s, under the population bomb and everything, and sort of arguing the case that it's a little bit more complex than simply that. Prosperity is driving fertility rates down and people are choosing to have fewer children. And again, it's part of this sort of fascist motive to promote larger families, which ultimately conflicts with what families want to do and you see right across the developed world where families are actually going to have fewer kids because they don't need to have large families. But it's a fascinating book. I encourage people to have a look at it. As usual, my views are controversial. I go against the narrative. I challenge assumptions, but I encourage people to think and try to work it out for themselves, and I provide them with a lot of different perspectives in the book, from an economic point of view, I look at Marx and Keynes, Adam Smith, and others. I encourage people to make up their own mind about this really important issue.

Hrvoje: I love a good contrarian. That's how I am myself. I think I'm just going to have to bite the bullet and buy all of your books in physical hard copy, if I can get that through, it's so weird being in Mexico, if it's not sent through the Amazon logistics system, it's not going to get to me. It goes into the big black hole of the Mexican corrupt and inept Postal Service. I managed to get one book today, a used book, I've been looking for, 50 bucks about world government from the 1980s. When I get your books, but I'm just curious though, I think you just mentioned about the Baby Race book again, something the opposite of what we're told. I'm like you, I'm very sensitive to fascism, to the possibility of us descending into fascism. So, I think this is good. We have to be, you know, be very sensitive to any moves towards fascism, but the logic is generally, you know, people like Musk and others say that we should have more babies like, that's a good thing, but are you saying that, and you know the elites, we tend to think they want to depopulate us. So again, what were you arguing?

Michael: Well, I'm arguing that there's no economic or social reason for large families. Ultimately, if you have a child, you have as many children as you want, that is your own personal choice, and people should be free to make that choice without government interference or without people saying you should have one child, five children or no children. Those choices are personal choices. And we should leave it at that. It is interesting. There was a politician in Australia, who was treasurer in the past, who promoted the idea of *'one but one for mum, one for Dad, one for the country.'* And when I was doing my research, I found another group of people were saying that a long time ago and they went by the name of the Nazis. And I actually found a very similar quote by one of those guys. And it's a shameful thing that a former Australian politician was promoting something that Adolf Hitler and his guys, and his mates were promoting back in the 30s. And so that's an interesting thing. The other interesting thing of course, is that behind the promotion of higher fertility is the sort of Marxist view. And goes right back to the labor theory of value, which was what Marx promoted. He said that labor power is the source of value, and that when the person is working and they're exercising their labor in the workplace, that that value is appropriated by the capitalist and is sort of the Marxist view and a lot of people believe that the more people you have the more productive society becomes, and this is actually a Marxist view that comes from Karl Marx and Adam Smith and his friends they all they started with the labor theory of value as well and they believed it until they thought no, this doesn't make any sense to us. And so, they moved onto the market and the invisible hand. And so, Marx's response was, *'Oh well, there is a conspiracy. Adam Smith and the others they had this plan to exploit the world.'* And so, he came up with his labor theory of value and unfortunately, if you read Capital, it starts off with a good idea, but he tried to create a mathematical proof for the labor theory of value, and that was the end of it. It doesn't make any sense, it's just complete nonsense, but really that is at the heart of contemporary discussions over low fertility, this belief that it is labor that confers value in society. But as you and I know, it's really the marketplace and that is what determines the value of a commodity in terms of value of the things being bought and sold. And so that's really the contest of ideas.

Hrvoje: I can get what you're saying. It's a very technocratic, you know, you can call it fascist, technocratic, for the state to get involved, that's population control, technocracy, scientific dictatorship. And you know, I just, you know, I think there can be room for nuance. I just read in Hungary they just said if a woman has four children now in Hungary, she won't have to pay income tax for the rest of her life. Again, interesting, I bet it would urge some people who otherwise wouldn't have four children, you know, to cross that Rubicon and have a fourth child. So again, I guess we're going to have to get the book and read it real quick. Michael.

Michael: I encourage you to do so and also just want to make a point when I was doing my research I came across a number of people, I interviewed a number of these family planners in East Asia who were, particularly in Taiwan who did a lot of work, in promoting family landing and you have to sort of see it from their point of view in the 50s and 60s, they were terrified at the collapse of their country because there were too many people. It sort of overflowed with people. And we now know that that really was a superficial understanding of the time. But I can't doubt their genuine sincerity that they felt they were doing the right thing and in hindsight, but we look back and say no, no, that was draconian, it was sort of the wrong approach and so on. When I spoke to these guys, they sincerely believed that they were doing the right thing and I think we have to be, we have to be cautious in condemning the past and saying, well, you guys are wrong and you're a bunch of idiots and so on. You work with what you have, and in a situation like the population explosion period of the 60s and 70s, there was genuine fear that countries like Taiwan and Korea were descending into chaos. Indonesia, of course, had their collapse leading to the rise of the Suharto and so on, so there was genuine fear, and instead of, I guess instead of the West trying to come up with a better program, they sort of forced this entire complex issue into the whole communist versus capitalist thing and they decided that anything that was against communism was good and would support it regardless of the consequences. And so, in Asia you have a very low birth rates and that is a consequence of very draconian family planning process in the 1960s and 1970s.

Hrvoje: Right. The book is *"Baby Race."* Freedommatterstoday.com. Check it out I'm sure on Amazon and elsewhere. Hidden Road Publishing. We gotta jump real quick. Michael, to our headlines. We'll be right back.

Hrvoje: We continue our conversation on this Rebel Transmission with semi-regular guest, Rev. Dr. Michael J. Sutton, out there in Sydney, Australia, his website, Freedom Matters Today, check out his books, and podcast, and so much is going on that it seems that every time we talk a new front in the 3rd World War opens up, and I'm afraid the next time we talk, what will we be talking about. Of course, we were discussing Ukraine and Russia and last time you were out there in Russia I was there six years ago.

I got to shake hands with the last Soviet President Gorby, now in Israel and Palestine. what sort of on your mind these days?

Michael: That's a really good question Hrvoje, and you say like every time we talk there is this avalanche of events amazing things we live in exciting times. I think that it's definitely a time that we look back on and say, wow, those times were remarkable. I wrote about what's happening in the Middle East, actually in my book. *'Is Russia Our Enemy,'* about a year ago I suggested that what's happening is this: since Trump was elected in 2016, there's been this factional dispute within the state in America and in other states over whether or not we should dispense with democracy and embrace fascism because the West is declining, and they see democracy and democratic rights as an obstacle to the continued prosperity of those states, and so from Trump onwards, we have to hate Trump and then we had to hate the unvaccinated and then we have to *Stand with Ukraine* and then perhaps next will be Climate Hysteria and *Stand Against China*. But I do write in my book that and perhaps one another, one other in the future, my feeling is that another Holocaust is coming. I wrote this last year, and my deep feeling is that fascism always has this interest in anti-Semitism, and it's always there in every fascist enterprise in history, there's always been these sort of antisemitism in Spain, in the exception probably is

Japan, when they when they rebelled against the Nazi directives to exterminate Jews. But in terms of European versions, Western fascism, there's always been this antisemitism but what's interesting about this one Hrvoje, is that unlike the Ukrainian conflict, almost immediately the *'Stand with Ukraine'* banner went up within a week, it was *stand with Ukraine, stand with Ukraine* across the West. And there was this very strange kind of complete deference to the Ukrainian side and then it's deleting the Russian narratives from the West. But this conflict is very different, because most people didn't know where Ukraine is, most people don't know where the Ukraine is or even Russia for that matter. But the Israeli conflict is an ancient conflict. This is about retribution, about vengeance, about payback, it is such deep thing. And what's happening is that there is no consensus in the West over what position to take some countries support is through some countries don't support Israel, they support Hamas. And what's happened is that the narrative that was promoted since Trump has fallen apart, the idea of fascism is you can't have an opinion, you must do as you're told. And the worst thing for this fascist experiment is that you have people who just don't agree on any aspect of this conflict. And so, you have 300,000 Israeli troops waiting on the border. Netanyahu doesn't what he is going to do, Biden doesn't know what he is going to do and there is complete confusion. And for the first time since 2016, there's this new dynamic People are having different points of view, the French sending warships to the Middle East to help Gaza, you have Australian prime ministers who refuse to take a side, in Sydney, they put the banners up on the Opera House and then there's protests about that. And then there's Bankstown Council putting up the Palestinian flag and there's all this debating and arguing, this is very strange because it goes right against this narrative we've had since 2016 that there is only one truth. And you're not allowed to have a debate. And so, it's very, very interesting I think, Hrvoje, what's happening in the Middle East because it is really a deep and ancient conflict, and I don't think it was ever part of the plan.

Some people have been saying, *'oh, this is part of the global conspiracy.'* But the reality is that in this part of the world and in many parts of the world vendettas, revenge, retribution, this is deep, ancient stuff. And people in the West don't understand retribution. They don't understand revenge culture. They don't understand this idea that is so deeply rooted in our DNA that it's something we can't defeat. We can't even understand it.

Hrvoje: I call it the original *'forever war.'* I was recently on a guest on one of my guest's podcast, Jeremy Ryan, shout out to him. He's got a great podcast and I, just off the cuff, I came up with that term, the *'Original*

Forever War,' Israel, Palestine. And you know, Philistines in Israel. And I actually recorded a podcast this afternoon with the former DOJ prosecutor who worked under Durham and who recently wrote a book trying to deal with these issues of genocide and terrorism and hate. And it's interesting. I never thought about that until you brought it up. How you know with COVID it's like everyone puts on their profile, the face mask icon, with Ukraine, everyone throws up the Ukraine flag with the rainbow fascism, on everyone throws up the you know the transgender LGBTQ Plus to Infinity flag and then with Israel Palestine. It's like there's a glitch in the system. It's like, you said, it's like some people for Palestine, some people for Israel, some people just back away like myself. I think you're onto something. And I think it's also important for people not to think everything is a conspiracy. You know, there's different extremes where the, the, the normies who don't believe anything is a conspiracy and then the other extreme is everything's a conspiracy and there are as you mentioned organic geopolitical like all throughout history you know struggles, wars, the desires of empires, or would be emperors and so there is an organic factor when you say another Holocaust. Well, I mean, I can't in my mind visualize like what that what, what do you mean like you think the Arab states would gather against Israel or what are you sort of alluding to?

Michael: It's hard to know with history, it's hard to know, but I do feel that there is another Holocaust coming and there's always been antisemitism in the West. Its deeply engrained in our culture tragically, even though Christ was a Jew, and his message was one with all are one in Christ neither free nor slave, male or female. And that's been the gospel message that Jesus has come to bring, I guess unity among the races and all the people but despite the teachings of Christ and the teachings of Christianity, the church through history has promoted anti-Semitism and there has been a lot of persecution and we see the arrival of the Jewish state and the problems with the other children of Abraham, if you'd like to use that phrase, it is really a tragic indictment of the children of Abraham, because Christians, Jews and Muslim are unable to live together in peace in the Middle East. But I do have a fear. I do have a fear that we live in a world that, you can't get away with terrible acts of violence and the temptation, of course, when horrific things happen, as we saw with 9/11, is to lash out in violence against someone else. And I remember September 11, I was in Japan, I was, I was actually leading the church service. And I told the audience, I said, look, we really have to consider what we're doing here. If we don't, if we don't embrace Christ's teachings of forgiveness, or at least try to contemplate forgiveness, we will be at war in the Middle East for 20 years. And I was right. We were at war in the

Middle East for 20 years, and tragically, the thing about forgiveness Hrvoje, is it's awful. It's an awful thing to do, and it's about absorbing the pain of suffering and accepting that that the terrible thing that has happened is something that I'm prepared to accept. And, you know, for me as a Christian I struggle with forgiveness. But I do believe God enables us to receive the Spirit to enable us to forgive, because we have been forgiven by God in Jesus, but at the same time, forgiveness is the only path forward for the Middle East and these conflicts, the alternative, is just endless death and killing. And so my fear is that, if Israel goes into Gaza and the killing starts, we are going to see a lot of death, a lot of dead people, a lot of a lot of dead, and it's easy for people who sitting in nice, comfortable buildings in the Australia and America, you know, say, oh, what you should do is this, what we're talking about human life here. We're talking about is human life and the ancient creeds and religions of Christianity, Islam and Judaism believe that we have made in the image of God. And so, what we're talking about is killing people made in the image of God and there's nothing worse than murder, killing another person and you see it tragically in the lives of the soldiers who fight in war. They come back and they're expected to get on with life. But how can you once you've crossed that boundary, we need to walk with the people who fight for countries fight for their nation.

Absolutely. But why force these guys and these women to go down the path of death when in such a terrible thing.

Hrvoje: What came to mind for me was, you know, I yeah, I would agree with you as well. Forgiveness is the way. It's the most difficult thing. Maybe that's why because that's the correct thing to do. And again, I was having this conversation earlier with my other guest. I was using the example of myself being the Croatian, but then we've got the Serbs and there are still some Croatians today, who view Serbs as inhuman, the enemy and vice versa. I'm sure there are some Serbs that feel that way about Croats, but there are a majority that have moved on and I don't see, I view all Slavs as my brothers, you know Russians, Ukrainians, Serbs. Because if you go back far enough in history, we were all one big Slavic tribe that over time we broke off and our language is changed. But if you go back far enough in history, you know, we were all in, in one Slavic group. That's how I view it. But people today, well, you know when the Croats have to forgive the Serbs and vice versa. And then there are powerful stories and video clips people can find online. I've seen these in the past where you know, there was some murderer who killed the child or spouse in a Christian family, and people can find these and they're really like, it really makes you think for a long time where I've seen the Christian parents forgive the murderer in the courtroom for the murder of the child or spouse or whatever. And that will just sort of leave you speechless like wow, just to digest, you know, compute that in your mind that is just really an incredible. Its time, Michael for our break the Michael's website again is freedommatterstoday.com. He's got a bunch of books you can check out. A podcast and people are free to call in. We'll be right back.

Hrvoje: This is the final segment with Rev. Dr. Michael J Sutton, coming to us from Australia. I'm out here in cartel territory in Mexico. Earlier this week, 13 Mexican police were executed by 30 plus cartel members. Just another day here in the good, the bad and the ugly. I'm living in a spaghetti Western.

Again, Michael's website, freedommatterstoday.com, and we're talking about Israel, Palestine. I guess everyone's talking about that. And just one more thing to mention Iran. I feel that Western governments, this has been talked about for a long time, and the Pentagon has desired war, it's in statements of a number of officials. Wesley Clark has discussed this, the Bush administration, that they have had a plan to regime change, by hook or by crook, Iran. I just saw an insane clip today of Mitch McConnell talking about how all this money going to Ukraine is a great thing because that money for war in Ukraine is, a lot of it's going back to America to support the industries in America, so it's like saying, you know, war is a great thing because

Americans are getting rich from it. It's absolutely insane. So, I fear them going to war with Iran and then with that, it's just there are unforeseen consequences there.

Michael: Yeah, absolutely. Hrvoje, I agree with you that this warmongering is that it has no end in sight. What the West doesn't understand what killing other Europeans or what I suppose or people like is the Anglo-Saxon killing each other have a similar culture in a way. But when you cross significant cultural boundaries, you enter into an entirely different worldview, and I think the West has always had a revenge culture for centuries and a retribution culture every nation has that. But with the teachings of Christ and forgiveness that came about 1800 years ago or so, when it became part of the state, there's been this contest between forgiveness and retribution and sometimes retribution win, sometimes forgiveness has won, but we do see the always the possibility of forgiveness because as Christians, we're encouraged to forgive because Christ has forgiven us by dying on the cross for our sins. And so, for us we struggle with this as a Christian community and as a nation, we struggle with this as well by nations for whom forgiveness is irrelevant, it has no part to play, and when we go to war with nations where there is no real sense of forgiveness, what we are doing is, in a sense, setting ourselves up for a lot of misery in the future because they don't believe in *'forgive and forget,'* and they're not going to countenance that. But I do see a shift in America, as you probably have already over the years, that back in the 90s, it seems like a long time ago, there was a genuine effort after the end of the Cold War, there was this sense that peace and trade and economic development and everything was all going to work together for good. And we were all going to be doing this plan of prosperity and then somehow after 9/11, the shift happened, no, no, we are going to go down the path of war, war, and more war And that's where we are today, but I don't believe it's the end game. I believe that there is this contest within the state between the old traditional view which we can cooperate and this new view, which is about conflict. TNT Radio is working, alive and well, and the Brownstone Institute is there as well. The fact that I haven't been arrested in Australia, that this contest is alive, and hope is alive. And that's what's so fantastic about this time Hrvoje, is that hope is alive, its not sliding into fascism and complete totalitarianism. Where there is still hope, and the more we promote it and talk about alternative perspectives, the more chance there is for a better world, and a better society for us, for our children and grandchildren.

Hrvoje: I think that's a very important point that you just mentioned that we are at the height of this struggle now and you have many principles. I always view, I don't think about whether we're going to win or not. My view is always looking at stoicism, you know, the art of manliness, all this sort of stuff. It's our duty to test our metal or grit to fight for truth regardless of whether we're going win or not, so we must participate. We, as Teddy Roosevelt said, you know, we have to be the man in the arena, get, you know, get in the arena and what you just said, we always have to keep hope alive.

I listened last night to a sermon from a fellow Croatian, American Paul Washer, well known preacher I am a big fan of that he was talking about, he was using one example that if you eliminate hope it's over that there has to be hope and you know he was speaking more in spiritual terms, but he said, if you know if I had some task to do and if I don't have any hope I'm not going to do it, but you know if I see hope in it, I will work 100 years towards that goal. You know if I believe that there's some hope. And so there are people getting down and dejected. But you know, I asked that to Ron Paul. He kept me going. He's 88 years old and he just keeps going. And I was like, you know. If he can do it. Just the fact that he's there at 88 going like the Energizer Bunny, that alone keeps me going. And so, you know, any other thoughts? And then as well as Covid now know I've had on recently this week a former attorney, I think lawyer, retired policeman who's working on opening investigations criminal investigations into the Covid crimes. So of course, there's still the Covid stuff that's lingering. And so, you know that or any other thoughts?

Michael: Well, it is interesting because in Australia we're being I guess, celebrating the defeat of the referendum, which again was part of this fascist narrative that we're going to have a Referendum, Hrvoje, but you're only allowed to vote *'yes.'* And so, if you have wanted to vote no, you house was vandalized your car was scratched, there were no *'No campaigns,'* anywhere because they knew that they would be bullied or harassed. But the Australian people voted overwhelmingly to defeat the Referendum, and I think this was a litmus test against the fascism that we've had in the last 10 years. What it is, is a middle finger to the narrative which has been that you're not allowed to have a choice and the average person, I don't believe it's the average person, they're not stupid, they're being manipulated and lied to, and I guess pressured and persecuted. But at their heart they just want what everyone in the world wants, they want to be safe, they wanna be happy. They want a good life for themselves and their family. And they just want to be left alone to think for themselves, and in a sense that's what's democracy is, it is the freedom to have a life where you are allowed to make the decisions you want to make after yourselves and your family. And I think what's wrong with that and the fascism that we've experienced in the last 10 years or so is that you have to sit down and shut up and do as you're told and I don't believe that that's the only narrative in the state. I do believe there are a lot of people in the ruling class who believe in the old ways in the old status quo, and there is this contest that's going on and we see it played out around in every country. And the fact that almost every politician who promoted Covid Hysteria has left the scene for various reasons usually. Usually, *'Oh, I've I want to consider health reasons, or my family needs me or it's time to leave.'* But I do suspect there is a counter movement underway, and this is what's really exciting today. If we weren't allowed to talk. And if we were shut down or Brownstone Institute wasn't here, or if there was the one view with the current Israeli Gaza conflict. It's a terrible thing what's happening in Gaza, terrible thing. But it is an ancient conflict. And I think we do that part of the world a disservice if we try to simplify it. There are legitimate grievances on both sides, this is a painful, painful, terrible part of the world, with a lot of suffering and we really do as a community, we society, we need to work together. We need to talk; we need to share experiences and we need to act with a spirit of forgiveness because God has forgiven us. We need to, we need to swallow the pain and the suffering, and we need to at least try to forgive, and I think the path forward Hrvoje, is simply talking to people with whom you disagree and sitting down, maybe over a beer or coffee and say, *'look, I don't understand the world from your point of view.*

Tell me about your point of view and let me listen to you. Let me hear. Let me tell you my point of view, and let's try to work this through.' And I think that's really the only way forward in a civilized society.

Hrvoje: I mentioned this quote earlier, Vala Afshar said to strongly disagree with someone and yet engage with them with respect, grace, humility and honesty is a superpower. I'm just going to also mention that you mentioned the Covid era politicians disappearing over the weekend. I came across my governor here in Mexico and an event, and he was just walking alone with his kid. I could have gone up to him and during Covid I was constantly commenting on his tweets. He was pushing the lockdowns, floating ideas like checkpoints to enter or exit the state internal Soviet passport system here in Mexico or changing the state constitution to allow forced vaccines. None of that happened. They were floating those ideas. And I thought about going up to him and asking him like, *'Who is really giving you those orders? Because they know you. You were, you know, following international orders.'* But then I just kind of looked at him. He looked kind of pathetic. I was tired, and I'm just kind of like, whatever. You know, I'm kind of like moving on. And so yeah, we're down to a minute left. I did want to ask but we ran out of time about the No Vote. I'm not as well versed on that. I'm sure my other Aussie colleagues are, my assumption is that was a related to a UN globalist plot the vote out there in Australia, but I guess we can talk about that next time again, Michael, tell us the best places to find you and your latest projects.

Michael: OK, it's freedommatterstoday.com. I also have a podcast which is broadcast every Monday morning. The current series is looking at the identity of Jesus, who is Jesus and is under the theme of freedom from past and prejudice and I encourage anyone who is interested in in God or interested in Jesus to have a have a listen to that. And you can find my books on hiddenroadpublishing.com or on my Amazon author page and we have our slogan is remember freedom and the survey because you matter to God. That's really important. Everyone matters to God and God sent Jesus to give us true freedom.

Hrvoje: Alright, until next time. Thank you, Mike.

10
28 November 2023

Interview with Hrvoje Moric, on 'The Hrvoje Moric Show, TNT Radio

https://tntradiolive.podbean.com/e/michael-sutton-on-the-hrvoje-moric-show-28-november-2023/

Topics: Covid Hysteria, Faith and Life, Fascism.

TRANSCRIPT

Hrvoje: Returning to the Rebel transmission is our semi regular guest now, Rev. Dr. Michael J. Sutton, political economist Professor Priest, Pastor, now publisher, CEO of Freedom Matters. Today. He's got a number of books you can find everything at freedommatterstoday.com. Welcome back to TNT Radio.

Michael: Thank you very much, Hrvoje, wonderful to be with you.

Hrvoje: Because it's your first time on videos, people can see you now as we are now in our second week of live video transmission, which has been fun, and so, yeah, how are things, there's a lot, you know, I think we're going to cover, you know, all the international conflicts happening now, Israel, Palestine. Ukraine and also get your thoughts on the recent developments in Australia regarding the Voice and then the conference as well that recently finished. So, how are you, and where would you like to start?

Michael: I'm very well thanks Hrvoje, asking and thank you again for having me on your show. It's really great to be with you. I'd like to start with the conference that I attended. It was a great conference. It was the inaugural Australians for Science and Freedom, conference, trying to do in Australia a little bit like Brownstone in America but on a much smaller Australian scale, I suppose. What I found interesting was lots of great speakers from various backgrounds, walks of life and Covid Hysteria brought us all together and it was a really interesting experience because of that, it's not the old sort of, the old coalitions and alliances have broken down over Covid Hysteria. And so, people who would have nothing in common in the past are brought together by Covid Hysteria and have this common cause and common trauma, I suppose, and that's what I reflected upon in the conference. And it was interesting because so many people who spoke are suffering from this as I am, and you are, as millions of people around the world have this Covid trauma. And it's not long Covid. It's nothing. There's always going to be some kind of sickness. But what we've experienced is this traumatic experience and so many people there and so many people in the United States and in Mexico, probably around the world lost their careers, lost their jobs, lost their reputations as a result of this experience. And so, there's, there's that negative side, but on the other side, there's new opportunities, there's, in a sense, a coalition of disparate voices all working together and there's new, there's new alliances being formed like a counter revolution like TNT Radio, Freedom Matters Today, Brownstone and the Association for Science and Freedom working together to, I guess, provide a counter narrative to what's being shoved down our throats. For me, my debrief, I had a debrief for the conference, my debrief was that, unfortunately not much has changed politically in Australia. There is an interesting thing that almost every politician who was pushing Covid Hysteria has been forced from the scene which I raised the question how is this possible and how is this magical formula implemented that so many politicians in the prime of their career and some of them were very young? I mean, they're in their 40s, politically, they just left for a variety of reasons, and they all have one thing in common. They all were pushing vaccine mandates, vaccine passports and so on. So, I find that very interesting and no one can explain to me why that occurred and why this is continuing to occur. The other, the other thing that struck me was that beyond Covid, there is a fragmented movement. TNT is able to transcend that, and Freedom Matters Today, I'm much broader than Covid Hysteria, but what I found interesting was we were, the conference was taking place in the context of missiles being flown into Gaza and tanks blowing up buildings. And it was sort of surreal in a way because and not only that, there's the conflict in Ukraine. And we're talking about Covid Hysteria, but yet the same dynamics and politics are present in these two conflicts in terms of indoctrination and propaganda. And we were never, we weren't even talking about it. But it did remind me, and I think I suspect probably behind, that is a lot of the attendees were academics from an academic background. There is a bit of a kind of an Ivy League, no Ivy Tower, monastery kind of feel of academia. I attended a conference during the pandemic in the middle of the lockdowns, and there were hundreds of presenters, thousands. There was an International Studies Association conference online, but nobody talked about the pandemic. It was as if it was not even happening. And I find that just astounding. And for me that that kind of dissonance between reality and kind of our reimagined reality, I think it probably goes to the heart of what really is the chief problem for us today. And that is we live in a society where terrible things are happening, but we can quite easily just literally turn off and want to have nothing to do with what's happening.

Hrvoje: There's a lot of interesting things there, I mean just this last comment that you made about, turning things off, I actually had that thought this morning, that I think was Israel, Palestine, and Gaza. And I know for everyone, everyone's got their own personal focus, for me, right now, that's not my personal focus. You know, maybe a few weeks ago, it was. I'm looking at other issues, but I just thought was like in my feelings. There's just a lot of Israel, Palestine stuff and I thought I would just think that I can kind of turn down the top of the volume on while look at other stuff and then you know, maybe next week I'll turn it back up, you know, definitely, Elon Musk was with was with Netanyahu and Israel over the weekend, so, you know that's an interesting development and it's funny, apparently I read about dictator, Dan was not welcome to become a member of a Golf Club did you get that?

Michael: No, no, I didn't. But I'm not surprised. He was a very controversial figure.

Hrvoje: Mike, Are you back again? There seems to be

some sort of interference...

Michael: I see a pattern and I believe that there is a pattern going away along and that is that's been going for many years and that is sort of setting us against each other. But at the same time there is a pattern Covid Hysteria, the election of Trump Covid Hysteria, the war in Ukraine, the war in Israel is all in a sense, the same kind of dynamic, and it involves the demonization of a particular group of people, the imposition of a singular narrative, and also, it's the desensitization towards what really is horrific destruction, the destruction of Covid, the destruction of lives in Gaza, destruction of lives in this Ukraine, conflict with Russia, that's been going on for years. But it's sort of a continuation of that and what it does is to us, if you remember back to the Bosnian conflict, of course you would, but for weeks and weeks and weeks and months, we would desensitize to what was happening there. We knew every night there was another news story about it. And we were just desensitized to what was going on to the point, really where people just turned off, and so this is where we're going with this conflict and these series of conflicts. And I feel that probably the end goal is to promote, I guess, an indifference in society so when America finally goes to war against China, we won't have a problem with the carpet bombing of cities, and the decimation of infrastructure in the same way that we kind of were indoctrinated in World

War 2 to accept Total War, which was the destruction of German cities, Japanese cities and so on. And we look back and say, *'oh, it was terrible what happened in Hiroshima.'* It was. But the carpet bombing of German cities, British cities, Coventry and in the course Japan and that generation was desensitized in the same way we are as well. And I think there's definitely a difference, not a conspiracy, but there is a deliberate process underway, and the goal of course is to ensure that America stays on top. But history always has a way of unearthing, God, in a way behind orchestrating is his way is not our way, and we often think that we are orchestrators of our own destiny. But I think history will prove that that's not true once again.

Hrvoje: That's a great point. I would agree with you. I feel they are going to take us to war with China. But the question might be what sort of war, it may not be some all-out war, it might be a series of limited war, but as you say they have been desensitizing us, normalizing all these things we are seeing now, the horrors, it, traumatizing us. All these things that we're seeing now, these horrors traumatizing us, and you know the entire entertainment industry has been participating, you know, violent video games and films and the news cycle just we are bombarded daily from anywhere you look, whether it's news or video games or TV shows. I mean there is, I'll be somewhere, and I don't have a TV, but I'll be somewhere where maybe I'll catch, there's a TV on and there's a TV show playing and it's just people just murdering each other nonstop, and I'm just thinking, how is that, you know, edifying or a normal thing?

You think about. In history past, I mean, people were not exposed to, this is not a normal thing, could just be, you know, I saw some skit from like, a comedy skit this morning on a telegram, and it was funny. They were mimicking that one of those, you know, the chef TV show where they, they get fired, and in the end the chef stabs the contestant, and I'm like, that's not funny, that's crazy. But you know, moving on also the Voice Referendum, your thoughts on that as well as people who are not in Australia, you know if you could tell us what the greater importance of that was.

Michael: Well, that's a really good question, Hrvoje. The Voice Referendum was defeated soundly, and I believe that behind it was that Australians don't like being told what to do. And it was again this singular narrative idea that we're going to have a vote, you're free to vote, but you must vote yes. And so there is this attitude of the government, and it was defeated effectively, what it was going to do was to give a small group of people political power, unlike which they've never had before, which was the idea was that aboriginal people were to have extra political power on any issue that related to them, and unfortunately, that sounds great. But that could mean absolutely anything and what it would do effectively in practice would be to enshrine an imbalance within our democratic Constitution. The other thing Hrvoje, I think that most commentators are not looking at it and it's happening in America as well. That's why Black Lives Matter started and Black Lives Matter and also the Voice referendum had one thing in common and that is that in America there was a period of time, I think 2017, or around about that time when the number of Hispanic Americans outnumbered the number of African Americans. And so, in terms of a political grouping, they were more powerful and so a lot of African Americans felt, oh, no, our power is going, we have to promote Black Lives Matter. Well, all Americans matter, of course, and in the same way, in Australia, Aboriginal people were terrified, many of them in power, who have benefited from the state-led slush fund that many of these bureaucrats have had for years and that is that migrants are increasingly identifying as Australians. So, 1/3 of Australians are born overseas and so this terrifies the old I guess, welfare lobby. Of course, there were the poor Aboriginal people as well. And there was a giant gravy train for Aboriginal leaders that has now come to a halt because there are lots of migrants in Australia who need help. There's 11,000 Ukrainian migrants and every dollar that goes to them doesn't go to the Aboriginal slush fund. And so, the political elites, these aren't Aboriginal people, these are the Aboriginal political elites, they've made a fortune from, I guess, promoting the suffering of their own people. They promoted this Voice referendum to secure their political power. And it was a very clever ploy, but unfortunately the Australian people saw through it and voted against it, and it gave me great hope because I believe that the average person doesn't believe in fascism. They believe in freedom, and they want to be free, and we saw this this vote was sort of a middle finger to the political establishment, but it will be interesting to see what happens in the future.

Hrvoje: That, yeah, that reminded me what you said, you know, these Aboriginal elites and then the city elites and, you know, even the PLO like the Palestinian elites. And I, you know, I've heard, one of my professors back in Geneva was Yasser Arafat's brother in law, and it wasn't from him, but I just heard things, people who were closer to the developments in Palestine, going back, that you see a lot of these Palestinians, you know PLO elites driving a Mercedes and helicopters and you know, living the good life, not really doing much for the people they're supposed to represent. We saw the same thing with BLM, the few leaders of BLM really not carrying out their mission. And I guess that perhaps would have been similar in Australia. And then these elites, it's basically buying all the you know, the globalists in league buying off these elites to do their bidding. You talk about fascism. There was a fantastic thread recently, maybe to get your thoughts on this Cynical Publius on Twitter, this thread sort of exploded and he recently said five days ago. *"I'd like to explain why it's important that we call Democrats fascists and not Marxists."* He basically, he goes through the thread and that, he says, *"it's a winning tactic because the Dems and the leftist Liberals today the useful idiots, let's say of the globalist regime in power in Washington, they call everyone fascist. When you call them Marxist, they don't really care so much, but if you call them fascist that really gets them going,"* and I think he's got a point here because technically we could call like the Democrats, in Washington, fascists, because they're doing, they're working with the corporations to carry out this authoritarian agenda, any thoughts there?

Michael: Yeah, well, I absolutely agree. I think we have to be very careful when we talk about fascism because it's if we use it all the time to everyone, then the meaning of the word sort of is diluted and its effectiveness is taken away and we need to really be careful what we're talking about with fascism. But in the same way Marxism I, I also have a problem calling the left Marxist or even the term cultural Marxism I studied Marxism at University and was well trained in Marxism, Marxian economics, and I really don't understand what cultural Marxism is. It's certainly not Marxist. It's not Neo Marxist, certainly from the guys I studied at university, they were around the 70s and 80s. I would say it's sort of a layman's, layman's misappropriating an important concept. I mean there are there are a lot of Marxists around who've written some great stuff on what's happening in Gaza and also what's happening in Ukraine. And so, I don't doubt their commitment to the cause of justice and peace from their own perspective their own way of thinking.

I think we need to; we need to come together with people. We cover particular issues and realize, OK, yes, they may be on the opposite side, but they are saying some really good things and they're on the ball with this and a number of left-wing journalists have been killed in in Palestine and in Ukraine trying to report the news, trying to get the truth out. And we have to salute those who fight for their country, regardless of whatever political persuasion they have, whether they're left wing or right wing, the idea that someone wants to fight for their country, be it in Mexico or America, Australia, or China, it doesn't really matter what their political philosophy is. If they're prepared to die for their country and fight for their country, I always respect that.

But absolutely the left in Australia is fascist. I wouldn't call them Marxists. Marxists implies a degree of suffering, exploitation and also a lot of poverty. There was always, certainly in the old days, the Marxists were poor, they were fighting against the system. But in Australia and in America a lot of the Left are establishment figures. They're very wealthy, they're very well off. So, to call them Marxists is a little bit like calling them poor. They're certainly not poor, and they use political categories to promote values that they have no intention of believing in or following. And so, in a way, you know, all the candidates for the presidency in America, they're all wealthy people. They're all part of the elite. And so, it doesn't matter what they say, they do represent a section of society that Americans can't relate to, but we all, you know, we all look up to these people as being, I guess, symbols of the working class. But they don't know what the working class is about, even if they may have had some connection to it five generations ago.

Hrvoje: Yeah, there's a clip that I just came across somewhat juxtaposed some of Obama's statements from Vivek Ramaswamy and he's literally using some of the same recycled talking points as Obama and that kind of tells me it's like, you know, the fact he is Obama. 2.0. The second coming Nikki Haley is, you know, Hillary Clinton, you can't fool us. It's just more of the same. That I did wanna treat again from Cynical Publius as he says. That the, *"the then the Democrats and the Liberals America* *despise being called fascists, especially when you can explain cogently and accurately how they behave just like 20th century fascists regimes, they hate it because deep down they know it's true when they feel trapped on something when someone calls them on it, it embarrasses them and makes them act rashly and disempowers them, just like showing a mirror to a vampire. Please get on the board of Democratic Party is a fascist train, it's a winning formula.'* Alright, we're going to jump to our break Michael's website. Freedommatterstoday.com, we'll be right back.

Hrvoje: It is our final segment with Rev. Dr. Michael J Sutton of Freedom Matter Today, he's got a podcast and a Number of books. *Baby Race*, also the *Curse of Crooked River, The Third Tsunami, Monkey and the Castle by the Sea, Is Russia Our Enemy* and many more Freedom from Fascism. Before getting your further thoughts on, say, Israel, Palestine, Ukraine, China or anything of that, we were talking about Covid trauma. You know, any other thoughts on that? I think there are still people all around us. You know, I'm here in Mexico, wherever people are, some of our family, friends and neighbors, you know to different degrees where we're all nursing our wounds to this tyranny that we went through, some of them literally I, you know, I recently spoke to a Mexican who was twice injected and he was worried, wondering like what can I do? And I said, you know, first of all, relax, don't freak out. You haven't felt any effects so far. So, you, you may have gotten a placebo and, you know, look for detox protocols. So, there are people dealing with that trauma and well before, I guess I'll let you get to that, Michael. We do have a call from Joe who's got a question for you. Go ahead, Joe.

Listener: From the Christian perspective: what's your red pills? And you know about the unbelievable, unspoken evil the American Empire has done? You know over, you know, and going back to the Philippines in the 1800s. And all that. From the Christian perspective, is it is now, I know you don't believe in karma, is it better for your soul's betterment, to extricate yourself from this wicked empire?

Michael: Yeah, thanks, thanks, Joe for your question. I think that the Bible teaches us that we've all sinned and fallen short of the glory of God, and we are all the recipients of the grace of God found in Christ. I think also that we all are people who are made an image of God, but it's marred by sin, and Jesus has come to set us free from our sin by his death on the cross. And I also believe that we all it doesn't matter how far we've fallen or walked away from God. It's never too late for anyone to come back to God and we see this in the life of the apostle Paul, who was a murderer, probably a terrorist, we would call him a terrorist today, a little bit like Osama bin Laden in a way completely unhinged for much of his early life and probably a thorn in the side to the Jewish community as much as the Christian community. But God found him and changed him and made him into the man that he wanted him to be. And I think there's always the chance for evil people once they encounter God or God encounters them to change. As for evil empires, we do live in this world, and we can make an impact on the lives of people we know, and we love around us. And we have to remember that really God expects nothing more from us except to follow Jesus in the life that we have and to help bring that love of God found in Jesus to everyone we meet.

As for rising and falling of nations, we know that everything comes to dust. If you want to see the future of the American empire, go to a museum and you'll see what will happen to it. Everything turns to dust, but we are accountable beings and God gives us a wonderful opportunity in this, I guess as you say, evil empire to show a different path and you know people like Hrvoje, and others at TNT Radio doing a fantastic job in in applying their faith and their understanding to this world and trying to promote an alternative. I don't think that anything is too far gone because God is always there, even in the darkest of places.

Hrvoje: ...I don't think the answer is to plug out to some bunker. I think it's you know it's the American empire, there's plenty, you know, a lot of people who should stay,

stay where you are. You know, I always like to repeat Teddy Roosevelt's Maxim: do what you can with what you got. Where you're at, you shouldn't just flee from the empire. I mean, we're, we're now in a world empire. There's nowhere to escape. To you know. It's a global Soviet Union for the first time in history, basically and it's like it was my personal life circumstance that I somehow ended up in Mexico like that Red Hot Chili Pepper song *'Soul to Squeeze,' there I go. I just don't know. I might end up in Mexico,* and so I just my circumstance doesn't mean everyone should leave because, yeah, you know that's not running, is not the answer I had David...on recently. He's a former Canadian forces veteran...his parents fled Communism and his father said now he wouldn't live anywhere if he were in Croatia still today or Canada, where he is now, he's not going to move because there's nowhere to escape to. We're in one global, globalist empire, two minutes to midnight. Michael, other thoughts, Israel, Palestine, Ukraine. Anything else?

Michael: Well, I just want to tell everyone about my upcoming book called the *Identity of Jesus or God's Pronouns*. We have to take the fight where we can and go back to the Bible and see things from God's perspective. That's what we do at Freedom Matters Today, look at things from a Christian perspective. We have to open the Bible, read it, and let God speak to us, and sometimes he says things we don't want to hear, but we grow through that, and we grow through those that exchange with God, a conversation with God, and I think we need to be honest with God, with our lives and with each other and as you say, the journey starts here, Hrvoje, it's about what we can do following Jesus, where God, wherever God sends us. And so, I just encourage your listeners to do that and to keep our eyes open.

Hrvoje: Surprised that you've got yet another book, you are a very prolific writer. How do you do it?

Michael: I can only do it with God's strength Hrvoje, God inspires me to write. I sometimes just spend like an hour, and it all comes to me as various articles and so on. But God's given me a gift to write. I've actually got five titles coming out in the New Year, a few more novels next year but, but *God's Pronouns* is good and also *Freedom from Fear* will be my next upcoming sequel to *Freedom from Fascism*. But we have to make a difference and we can make a difference. We follow Jesus each day, wherever he leads and like all the disciples, just 12 men changed the world. And there are definitely more than 12 men following Jesus today, so we can definitely make a difference. And thank you for your work Hrvoje.

Hrvoje: Well, thank you for yours and for coming on. I'm going to have to one of these days, get all of your books in hard copy. Just figuring out figuring out a way how to get them shipped to Mexico, because if I'm not careful they they'll just disappear in a big black hole. All right again. Let us know the best website, and place to get your books.

Michael: It's freedommatterstoday.com and they're all available through Amazon, check out my author page, subscribe to the blog podcast every Monday morning. We're looking at the identity of Jesus. It's a very, very thought-provoking series and hiddenroadpublishing.com as well. Got eight titles and five coming out next year, but to spend great booking with you Hrvoje and talk to you next time. God bless.

Hrvoje: Yeah, soon. And I like your optimism. And as you say, you know what we do matters. So, let's you know, keep on fighting the good fight with a smile on our face against this insane generation.

11

19 DECEMBER 2023

Interview with Dr Vic Dalziel Podcast,

https://rumble.com/v41v8l2-community-leaders-episode-4-dr-michael-j-sutton.html

Topics: Japan, Christianity, Jesus, authenticity, faith, the church, shakuhachi, music.

TRANSCRIPT

Vic: OK. So, today's guest is Dr. Michael J Sutton, my 4th guest in the Community Leaders podcast series. Michael has been a priest, a professor, a political economist, publisher, and an author. Michael has worked in

Kyoto, Tokyo. Washington, DC, and Sydney and has one of the friendliest faces I've ever seen. In 2021, during the height of the Covid-19 pandemic, Michael started Freedom Matters Today and Hidden Road Publishing and this year has published 8 books, well done. The vision for his company is to create a viable and credible publishing alternative that challenges established media narratives, fight for freedom, and speak truth to power from both secular and religious perspectives. Sounds pretty good to me. Michael, welcome to the podcast.

Michael: Thank you very much, Vic. It's wonderful to be with you.

Vic: Yeah, it's good to have you here. Surviving the heat in Sydney?

Michael: I think so. It's been very hot the last few days, that's for sure, yeah.

Vic: You've beaten the Gold Coast, which is quite rare.

Michael: Yeah. It's just, it's unrelenting. And nearby one of the mains of the waters has burst. And so entire suburbs are without water for the next day.

Vic: When I smiled then, because I thought, oh, that's a good water slide for the kids in the street, but yeah, no water is no good.

Michael: No, that's true, yeah.

Vic: Wow, so I'm excited to chat to you today because it's almost like we had a bit of a psychic connection last week when we decided that we're going talk about your time in Japan because since then, and very unusually, for Australia, and even internationally, Japan has been in the news. So, the first time they're in the news, I noticed was the very rare protest because it is quite rare for the Japanese to protest and that was organized by the *'Japanese for Japan'* group. And then secondly, I don't know if you saw it over the weekend, but Tucker Carlson released his podcast with Alex Jones, and they actually spoke about Japan in that podcast, which was extraordinary and so it came up in around the topic of Alex was talking about global depopulation and he specifically spoke about the declining birth rate in Japan and how by 2100 it's almost like there's gonna be no Japanese. So, it's really interesting that and I'm thrilled to have someone who has actually been in Japan for such a long period of time? You were there for a decade, living and working?

Michael: Yes.

Vic: It is actually quite rare to have someone, an outsider's perspective, or someone who has actually been on the inside, particularly in Japan for so long, because as I'm sure you're aware, but the listeners may not be aware I've done three months in South Korea and this is the only reason I'm aware of it is like South Korea and Japan and 97% homogeneous which is incredibly rare for contemporary society, and they also don't protest very much there and they do both have rapidly declining birth rates. So, what I thought we'd do is just and perhaps you could just start off by giving just a bit of a background about Japan, your time there and touch on any of the issues that I've brought up just now.

Michael: OK. Thanks, Vic, some great questions there and I think I'd have to say go on the record maybe for one of the first times Alex Jones might be wrong.

Vic: Right. OK.

Michael: It is interesting because Japan is not unique among developed countries. Japan, Korea, Taiwan and China, Italy, Spain, Portugal, they all have low birth rates, and this is largely a consequence of economic development, the evolution of capitalism, if you'd like to call it that, it's the, I guess, the end of children being seen as an insurance or parents in their old age. The provision of welfare for the elderly, the idea that we have here in Australia, where a lot of middle aged or older people have their own homes, they have their own assets, have superannuation. And they don't need to rely upon their children for survival. So, there's that factor. Another factor in Japan that's fairly specific to Japan was the idea of the American abortion policy that it was introduced, I think it was 1949. It might have been earlier than that, but the abortion policy was the most liberal in the world and has remained the most liberal. It was ironic that it was promoted by the United States, who recently overturned the Roe versus Wade decision and they were quite happy, happy to impose abortion policies on Japan but not impose it on their own people and as a result, millions of abortions took place between the late 1940s well into the into the early 60s, and so in effect, what happened because there was no real birth control, there was only abortion available to women. Abortion was effectively the main mechanism for fertility control and that is also quite remarkable. And so, in many ways, in some ways, Japan and China are similar in the sense that the One Child Policy was a strict policy and that effectively they estimate maybe 500 million Chinese were effectively prevented from coming into being during the One Child Policy and also in the previous policies from the 60s onwards. And so, in the same way Japan's current demographic structure is largely informed by the abortion policies of the late 1940s and 50s and so. That's had a huge impact on Japan. But with Japan is, as you say, like it's Japan and Korea, both 97% homogeneous in a sense, but it, but it even goes to a deeper and more controversial level than that. And we're allowed to talk about that here. I'm in Australia, you're in Australia. But if I was to talk about this in Japan, I would have to be very careful walking on the streets, particularly in some parts of Japan. Someone might knife me in the back.

Vic: I will say this. I can attest to that. So yeah, I was walking to a train station with a female colleague who was South Korean and for particularly older Koreans, it's that that's just not done. He assumed that she was my girlfriend. And so yeah, he just walked up and spat in my face and gave me a mouthful. So, it it's that for me, you know, being quite a naive Australian and also a wide Australian. I think it was the first time that I really kind of woke up to oh, OK, this is what racism can feel like for all people around the world, yeah.

Michael: Yeah, absolutely. And I think if you go abroad as an Australian, particularly a white Australian or an Australian with Anglo-Saxon heritage to many countries in the world, you see the world from a different perspective entirely. And you realize, wow, this is how minorities must feel here. Yes, and it shocks you to the core because you assume that well, I've always assumed that my values are the values which other people share and that a fair go for all and so on. But many people don't actually have that as a set of values, and so there's xenophobia that we experience in Australia towards Muslims or towards minorities is astounding. But it's even more astounding when you go overseas and you're on the receiving end of that as it is the equivalent form of racial discrimination simply because you're white. And so that's really a learning curve for white Australians going around the world as we learn about ourselves and learn about other cultures. But what I was going to say was that Japan is a nation of migrants, migrants in the same way that Australia is a nation of migrants and that's the most controversial thing you could probably say about Japan.

Vic: I've never heard of this before.

Michael: I mean the Japanese are an amalgam genetically of a variety of migration flows over the last 14,000 years or so, there's two groups. There are the Jomon people, which was a very long time ago. They were sort of the first settlers of Japan. Then there were the Yayoi people, and they're from Korea, three 300 BC. And they come from the three kingdoms of Korea. There were three ancient kingdoms in Korea's I can't remember their names, but you can Google it. And that's where the Yayoi people come from. And they are the ones who formed the ethnic basis of what we call the Japanese people today. There was also the Ainu, and there was another group called the Emishi, and they were the indigenous people of Japan. And so, a lot of those tribes were, in a sense, melded into the Yayoi people into the what became known as the Japanese people. When I hear something like *'Japan is for the Japanese,'* I immediately think *'well guys, you know. You know your ancestry is not Japanese. You come from Korea, you come from China, you come from India.'* This for me is not a terrible secret that must be concealed for me, but it is a wonderful heritage to be celebrated.

Vic: Yeah, wow.

Michael: If you, like I'm an Anglo Australian. My heritage is English, Welsh, Irish, Spanish and French. And I, rejoice in that incredible cultural heritage that forms part of my identity, and I don't know what part of me comes from those parts of my identity and what comes from me as me, and that's a journey that we all have to explore as human beings. What world do we create for ourselves? And what world do we inherit from others? But the Japanese with this *'Japan for the Japanese'*? They're in a sense, reinventing, reinventing a myth, which is that they're Japanese and they have nothing to do with foreign nations, whereas in fact their ancestry is from the mainland.

Vic: It's probably got more to do, I think, than with nationalism than like race, but I just, yeah, I love it when people breakdown because race has become such a strong identifier for people now and it is just a ridiculous notion when you think about the history, particularly the history that you've just given, that does give light. I had a Vietnamese colleague when I was in South Korea, and they were openly quite racist towards him. And I asked my manager why that is, and he sat me down and explained to me the way that Koreans see races and people from around the world and he said at the very top is Korea, and Japan and then everybody kind of falls in line underneath that. And a lot of it did quite stereotypically have to do with the color of someone's skin. So, does any do any of these issues that you've discussed? And thank you. That was amazing. And are they, did they come up in the book? You have written two books on Japan. I one of them is a novel and one of them I think you called the Baby Race. Is that sort of issues that you cover in those books.

Michael: Oh, absolutely. The *Baby Race* is a broad investigation of the issues that Alex Jones raises about the declining population in Japan and the prospects for what will happen in the future. But I don't just look at Japan. I look at Korea, I look at Taiwan and China and also America as well. I look at America. And Baby Race challenges the narrative, the challenge and the narrative is that a low birth rate brings about social chaos and economic decline. And so, what we need to do is have more babies and that that ties in with Peter Costello's famous statement: '*have one for Dad, one for mum, one. for the country.*' But he didn't realize was that the Nazi said, that too, I've. Got a quote in the book from one of one of Hitler's buddies, which basically is almost word for word, and it's kind of ironic in a way. What an awful thing to be associated with, that idea that women have to have babies for the country is, is obscene, politically incorrect, of course, but also economically irrational. And I show in my book, I look at 500 years of economic theory, and I show that mainstream economics has always rejected the idea that value comes from labor and labor power, and in fact value comes from the marketplace. And so, you could effectively run the economy with one person. You don't need millions of people to run an economy. Depending on what you're buying and selling, and so the ones promoting the labor theory of value if you'd like to call it that was of course the political economist Adam Smith and Ricardo and so on. They toyed with that for a while, but they rejected it and they decided to move to the market, being the source of value. Whereas our friend Marx, he thought, *'well, well, there is a conspiracy. They're obviously hiding something. They were talking about the labor theory of value, these wretched capitalists. And then suddenly they stopped talking about it, so there must be something there,'* so his idea was that the labor power of a person is what is appropriated by the capitalist and stolen. And that's the source of exploitation, so the idea is, the more children you have, the more value can be stolen by the capitalists, the more prosperous the society is. But the reality is, is that most economists have rejected that idea. And they talk often about the population pyramid, and they say, well, there are more elderly people than young people. The answer, of course, is adaptation to adapt to that reality. And the government has enough money to spend to solve those problems. If we can spend 300 billion on three submarines, that won't work, and it would be 3 submarines against the

100 nuclear submarines of China, it really is too much spending of that amount of money on that kind of thing and maybe we should be spending money on things that might actually benefit the average Australian or in Japan too. Japan has a very large military, even though the Constitution prohibits even the suggestion of the military, yes, so sadly, they're spending billions on the military and almost nothing on helping their own people.

Vic: Yeah. I'm not up on economic growth, but I know that whenever they're talking about having more children. It's about the constant growth model. So, you need more people and that is often an argument that's used for increasing immigration numbers into the country. You need a larger population because a larger population increases the base and keeps the money coming in and it needs to grow year on year, and also for some people they'll say that a large population is also about security and so on. Your model is a bit different from that. In the book, you said something there about it's based on a model where you could run an economy with one person, and I'm interested because I've often thought about just how grotesque this this constant growth and this constant need for growth year on year, whether it's just in a business or whether it's a country because of the outcomes of that obsession. So, I'm very interested to hear how it can be achieved. Or what the model is that you're referring to?

Michael: Yeah. OK. Well, I think the growth model has been largely questioned and discredited over the last 30 to 40 years, challenging ideas of GDP growth and per capita growth, and so on. There's been all kinds of formula to come up with more, I guess, more equitable understandings of economic growth. The point of the constant growth model, the idea of more and more migrants coming into this country, really depends on what kind of industrial structure we have. So, for example, in Australia, as in most industrial countries, there are many sectors of the economy where people are required to do to dirty, dangerous, and difficult jobs and so the young people of the eastern suburbs of Sydney won't be that keen on doing those jobs. They're more interested in, I don't know what they're interested in these days, but they're into…

Vic: I'd say podcasting, I'm joking, I'm from there.

Michael: But the funny thing is that all the Marxists, all the Marxists in the past, they were not poor people, they were not poor, Trotsky, Marx, Engels, Engels was a businessman, he ran a factory, so he was running a factory, which Marx was condemning in his book saying, ah, it's all about the factory system unlike my friend Engels who's running a factory, but it's obviously not quite the same, and so a lot of these Marxists were actually wealthy people, and in fact, all the economists in those days were members of the upper class and their understanding of the world was based on deductive reasoning, not empirical science, and so they've come up with a set of propositions and then try and prove them and reach certain conclusions. But empiricism really didn't, has never really been associated with economics. It's always been more of a more like a Sherlock Holmes kind of approach to the world, a deductive process. But getting back to the growth model, if you go to a country like Saudi Arabia or Singapore, there are a lot of people who are migrants who come in for short term employment. It's very dirty work, difficult work. They give money and send it back to their home country. It's an awful system in a way, that's the system that they decided to adopt. And they don't give many pathways for political enfranchisement, which is, I think, a great weakness for society. Society must always give clear avenues for political enfranchisement and social enfranchisement for anyone who works here. So, if someone comes here and they have no skills and they should have the right to become a citizen like everyone else, and if someone comes here with great skills, those skills should be recognized. Australia is a bizarre country in the sense that we recognize the skills of those who come from Great Britain, but we don't recognize the skills of those who come from India or Russia. So, you could be a fully trained doctor in Russia. You could have done thousand operations of the most difficult form, but you're just not recognized here, and you have been up cleaning the street and I find that unacceptable for a modern society. So, it's it does go back to the racism thing, the racism thing that we want the best jobs for ourselves, and we want the worst jobs for the newcomer. It's kind of like a generational racism sort of *'wait your turn'* racism. I use that term in in one of my books. It's this idea that mum and Dad well, they'll have a terrible life, but the kids will go to university. And I don't think that's the kind of society that we should have.

Vic: I think that is the society we do have though.

Michael: Yeah, it is. Yeah. Absolutely. Yeah. If that, and sorry if Vladimir Putin decided to give up his job and become a a become an Australian citizen is highly doubtful, he would be able to find employment given his qualifications because, you know, he didn't go through an Australian university he didn't get accredited by the unions and so there are all these bizarre stumbling blocks. But if you come from England or if you come from America, it's different, you're you get the fast track to the good job and that's of course it's the racism thing as well.

Vic: Yeah, of course. And I think it's the same if you come from any of the Commonwealth countries, probably or former Commonwealth countries, probably excluding South Africa. I wasn't expecting the discussion to go there. I might just dovetail for a second and now I told you I wanted to talk about Covid-19 because I've covered it from many different angles, perspectives, but not from a religious perspective, and I was wondering because you are a former priest, what your opinion as a religious individual.

Michael: That's a really good question. I think that I think you and I probably share many similarities of understanding how everything went. With Covid-19 and indeed a lot of the people within Australians for Science and Freedom, we sort of share a common understanding of the whole process, the issues and the events and the personalities and most recently, the last of the fascist premiers has gone. What a tragedy. What's interesting about a lot of these fascist premiers is that they have left in the prime of their career, which I find bizarre. They have many years of great public service they could give, and they've all departed the scene which is a blessing.

Vic: Correct me if I'm wrong, but it is incredibly rare for a premier in Australia to step down. Is that not?

Michael: It is, yeah.

Vic: Yeah. Yeah. And as you said, all of the ones that have done it have been really high in popularity with the general population and we're now in a position. Where we've had 4 premiers and one territory leader stepped down in the space of 18 months. I would say 18 months and it's a very unusual circumstance to see that happen. And as you touched on the commonality across all of them will, there's very little but other than they all from the same, are they all

Labor? Maybe. Yeah, I think so. But otherwise, is what the their draconian Covid policies and whether they know or have been told of something that's coming. But it does kind of give the sense that they're running a little bit running for the hills.

Michael: Yes, well, that's an interesting observation. I think there's a lot that must be going on behind the scenes about all of this because there's so many who are resigning and moving on and they all have one thing in common. They were at the helm when, when Covid Hysteria was at its height, and they were ultimately responsible for the nightmare that we endured. And the buck stops with them, really. But as a Christian for me, I have a different view to, as you know, to most of the Christians, many Christians in in Australia for me. For me, Covid Hysteria was the I guess the first real sign of the collapse of representative democracy into fascism, only to lurch back into a kind of regressive democracy, where we are today. So, we've had this this slide into fascism and now it's reversed back into this kind of regressive democracy. And it'll be interesting to see where it goes. But my contention is that fascism and democracy are like brothers in a way. Fascism is a natural consequence of representative democracy. So, in representative democracy we concede our power to others who act on our behalf. That's what representative democracy is, and that's basically what fascism is except it is a fuller version of the system where we voluntarily concede power to a person or to a group of people, and so it's natural that in the face of corporate power, the lobby culture in Canberra or Washington DC, I guess the two party system, the idea that the ordinary person really doesn't have much power anymore that fascism kind of takes over, and we saw it accelerated with Covid Hysteria. And then the churches, most of them, they the traditional ones, the Catholics, Anglicans and so on they all toed the line. They all did what they were told. They all were silent, and they all supported Covid Histeria, supported the vaccine, passports and everything, and the traditional view the conventional view is, *'oh well God wants us to do that.'* Well, God doesn't want us to do that. I can't find any text in the Bible that justifies that in fact, if you look at any of the great advances in history, the Christians involved in those periods of time were the ones who rebelled against the state because they felt that governments were challenging their conscience, challenging their rights and their freedoms. The American War of Independence was run by deists but also by a number of Christians. You have the civil rights movement in America that was largely run by people like Martin Luther King, a Christian pastor, the protest movements, overturning the Jim Crow laws, you have, even the Protestant Reformation, which is of course the result of which was a violent military revolution against the

Holy Roman Empire. And so, you have these pathetic, cowardly, spineless, gutless ministers in Sydney and Canberra and Melbourne and elsewhere say, *'no, no, we have to submit to the government, to do what the government says.'* The great revolutionaries of the past, who called themselves Christians, and who changed the world would be rolling in their graves and say, you are spineless, gutless cowards. And so, this is what happened and tragically that's the situation of the church.

Vic: Oh, wow OK.

Michael: That's the institutional church the Catholics and the Protestants and whatever; they've traditionally opposed democracy. They traditionally oppose freedom because they want the power for themselves. And so historically, they've never been on the side of freedom. They've opposed democracy at every turn. They've opposed movements of freedom at every opportunity. And so, it's not surprising for me that the church opposed it, didn't oppose Covid Hysteria. And what we have in Australia, Vic there are a number of people who are talking about how wonderful the church is and how wonderful the church was in Australia's past and how wonderful it was in Europe. And blah blah blah. Thank God the churches are not running the country anymore. Thank God! For 1000 years, the churches murdered their way through history. You and I would be dead if the churches ran this country. A great many other people would be dead too, and so we can't forget the fact that pretty much since Constantine, anyone who disagreed with the church was killed, and then we have the religious wars. We have the Protestant Reformation. These were not just spiritual revolutions; they were bloody violent revolutions involving the deaths of millions of people. And so, we have to remember that the church today wants that age where the church held the sword, the church still has its courts, they still have their ecclesiastical courts where they trial people in secret. The church doesn't believe in democracy or freedom. And that goes for all those fake Christian movements out there that are talking about Christianity and family and life and freedom, and democracy are completely opposed to that. Jesus came to bring his freedom not, religion, not religious power. It's completely opposite. Well, that's my position anyway.

Vic: But I just need to explain why I smiled halfway through what you said just now, and it was because for whatever reason, one of my young friends has told me you need to be more controversial on your podcast, like me specifically. And I'm like, well, I don't need to be because I can just bring Michael up to say those things because I would think that the vast majority of people like me, looking from the outside in would think that the church and the government the church is has been reformed and has embraced things like democracy. So yeah, that was good. I could really hear the passion coming through and voice and I know that we weren't gonna touch on this, but I did read when I was doing some background research on you about you. And I may be saying this wrong, but you talk about religion separating from the church? Is that what I'm saying, or you don't need a church in order to have religion,

Michael: Well, I talk about *'don't go to church, follow Jesus instead.'*

Vic: So right for a lot of people that would be quite revolutionary, because those two things are intrinsically tied for most people.

Michael: Yeah, it is. Goes back to what I what I wanted to say about Shintoism in Japan when I was in Japan, the Shinto priests they're the ones who practice in the shrines, and what they do is they have the ceremony where they bring the god out of the shrine, and they put him in a little box called a mikoshi and they carry the mikoshi around the Town, and this idea is, is the idea that the deity or the kami-sama, the god can be controlled, can be drawn out of his sort of resting place or his sacred space into the world we inhabit and then they carry the god around and they bless everyone. And then I realized when I was a priest and I was doing the Mass lifting the elements, if I might do it like this, you lift the elements and you say this is the body and the blood of Christ and in a sense, you are drawing God out of heaven. You're drawing the Holy Spirit out of heaven to these elements, and then you bless everyone in the congregation. You're doing exactly the same thing as they do in Shintoism, yeah, it's the same theology. And for me, Christianity is not about that. For me, God can't be controlled. God is God, like God is not a product of our manipulation and our power. God is beyond all that, and that God's presence, his presence on earth as Jesus shows us a different way to that religious power. And so, for me, my Christian faith is all about Jesus, his identity, his words, his actions, and wherever he goes, Jesus challenges the religious power of his day, and the religious power of his day is the same as the religious power of our day. And as soon as Jesus turns up to, if he ever turned up to today's church, they would crucify him all over again. You know, I often say that the 12 men or 12 disciples or 11 disciples, they changed the world. But in churches today, you can't change the light bulb without there being a huge fight or an argument about it. And churches they like to say you have to come to church to be a Christian. If you don't go to a church, you are not a Christian. But for me, understanding who God is through the Bible, finding about God and then following Jesus is all that we need to do. As Christians, it's not about going to church on Sunday, it's about a life. It's a lifestyle. It's an understanding of who God is and it's understanding about identity really, because I think that's really what Jesus is encouraging us to trying to get us to think about who he is and what it means to be a Christian. And you have the disciples who encounter God, and they spend the rest of their life trying to understand what happened. And I think for me, I believe Jesus is God and he's, my Savior. But it's still a journey of discovery. I don't have all the answers. I think that if you're walking, you know if someone has all the answers, they're on the wrong path and they're in the wrong place. So, it's interesting when I read the Gospels, when Peter the Apostle meets Jesus the first time Jesus tells him to follow him. He says, *'Follow me.'* And at the end of the story, right after all the things that happened, the death and resurrection, Peter goes to meet Jesus again and Jesus say, *'Follow Me,'* so it's the same thing and so and the question is *'follow you where?'* And Jesus will say, *'Come and see, let's go on that journey together. Let's see where we end up,'* and the early Christians were called *Followers of the Way*, which is very interesting. They weren't called members of the church, not even Christians. They were simply called Followers of the Way, those who followed a way, or a path through life following Jesus. And so, for me there's this distinction between religion and faith. Faith leads to God. Religion leads to the church. I'm not saying anything radical or new, unfortunately.

Vic: Well, I wanted to ask if there's a school of thought.

If people are listening to this, there is some long animosity and anger that's definitely directed towards the church. And I think even though I'm not a religious person, I do remember reading and hearing a lot about Jesus and what he did when he was alive, and I actually remember thinking, why is that so different to what religion is?

Michael: If I can follow up with that from my own my own upbringing, I always saw Jesus as someone I could follow. I couldn't understand half the things we did in church. I couldn't understand why we did certain things, why there were so many rules and regulations and so much anger. And I think for years, I wondered why people in church were so angry. And I think they're angry at God. They're angry at God, because they think that God is some kind of mean guy in the sky who wants to punish them, and I don't believe that's God. I believe God came to give us freedom, and that's what I talk about in Freedom Matters Today and I think that there's a wonderful, I guess, commonality we have when we read the stories of Jesus in that he lived the life that we live. And so, the idea of the Christian message is that God became one of us, not that we became God, and that God is one of us. He walked our life. He shared our experiences. And for me that sanctifies the human experience that says your life is beautiful your life is wonderful your Monday, and Tuesday, the rat race God is there too, whereas the church says, *'no, no, no, no,* *no all that matters is coming to church on Sunday, pay your dues, sing your songs, listen to the sermon, sit down and shut up and do it as you are told.'* And a lot of people just don't accept that anymore because they don't have to go to church. And for me, I'm interested in explaining things from a Christian perspective, trying to encourage people to see Jesus more clearly, I don't care about the church, whether it lives or dies. For me, it's about the identity of God. I've got a book coming out next week, actually called *'What are the pronouns of God'?*

Vic: That was the thought I was trying to get out before I was asking you about if there is. Book or text or anything that is on what you're speaking to, because I think it would be interesting to remove the idea of Jesus from the traditional text.

Michael: Jesus never wrote a book.

Vic: Is there is a book on what you're trying to articulate?

Michael: I've written the book *'What are the pronouns of God, the identity of Jesus from a Christian perspective,'* and in it I try to I try to communicate the identity of Jesus to people who, as you say, who are interested in God, but they just can't stand religion or the church, or they they've been abused by the church or bullied by the church, which is most people. Yeah. Most people have had a negative experience from the church. I can guarantee if you put 10 people from any suburb in Australia together and you ask for a common experiences, most of them will say something negative about the church, though some will say I like Jesus, but I just can't stand Christians.

Vic: And that I think that is a very, very, very common experience, so I was just gonna ask you about a quote from your website because it's fascinating and the quote is *"true Freedom is freedom from fascism and tyranny, freedom from fear and despair, freedom from sin and death, freedom from guilt and shame, freedom from war and conflict, and freedom from past and prejudice."* Well, what does that actually mean? Can you write that down? What does that actually mean?

OK, so I wanted to give freedom, a bit of coverage to relate to issues that are important to us today and it was during Covid Hysteria. And so, I was interested in freedom from fascism and tyranny, which is what we were experiencing. Then I thought, well, fear and despair, that's sort of related to that because we live in a fearful society and so on. And then I thought about, what does, I guess Christian freedom speak about? It speaks about freedom from sin, freedom from death, freedom from guilt and shame. And there's, you know, as you know, probably with Asian cultures, some cultures are sort of more shame-based cultures and other cultures are more guilt-based cultures. And so, we have to take guilt and shame together as two different approaches to, I guess the feeling of helplessness. Freedom from war and conflict was, it was added as a result of conflicts in our world and freedom from past and prejudice. And so, for me, I wanted to give a give a breadth to Freedom Matters Today. And people say, what do you, what sort of freedoms are you talking about? And these are the freedoms that I'm talking about. So, it provides a basis for a research program. I thought that I could cover all of them within a year, but I ended up doing freedom from fascism for all of 2022 and yeah, so it's taking a bit of time to get through all the all the themes, but the three Bible verses that inspired freedom matters today. One was from John 8: 36, which was, *'if the Son sets you free, you should be free indeed,'* and also Galatians 5:1, Paul says, *'it is for freedom that Christ sets us free,'* and he also says in 2 Corinthians 3:17, *'where the Spirit of the Lord is there is freedom.'* And so, for me, these three verses talk about freedom. And I thought, wow, this is great. This God wants us to have freedom. And then I went to the churches, and they said, *'no, no, no. We don't believe in freedom. It's submit to the government, submit to the Covid passports,'* and I thought, well, there's something wrong here. Either the Bible is wrong or you're wrong. And I think it's probably that they're wrong. And then there was the perverse Job-Keeper slush fund extension to churches where they changed the employment status of the ministers, pastors and priests to allow them to receive Job Keeper which was a scandal. And so, if you remember your Royal Commission into child sexual abuse, the church said, *'under no condition can we change the terms of employment of the priest. The priest is not an employee of the church, the priest is self-employed, we can never change this,'* they said, under no circumstances can this sacred position be changed, then along came Covid Hysteria, and then they change the term of self-employee to employee so, the priests and ministers and pastors could receive Jobkeeper. Interesting God moves in mysterious ways. And then once Covid Hysteria was over, they changed it back again. And of course, you know, they've come back to the same position: *'This is a sacred position. You can't challenge us. We are self-employed, we are not employees of the church.'* Yeah, right. For me, that was a disgrace. So, for me, it meant that the money that ministers pastors and priest received was more important than the compensation that needs to go to the victims of child abuse. And the church is wiping their hands and laughing all the way to the bank.

Vic: You said that you only managed, so you've done eight books in in one year. Is that based around this, this philosophy that I just articulated?

Michael: Yes, *'Freedom from Fascism,'* was the first one. And then *'Is God on America's Side?'* was about

America. I was just sick of hearing all this American stuff coming out of American theology, talking about how God's on American side, and so that book is, I guess, a critique of what you might have heard as Christian. Nationalism, very popular in Australia too. Yeah, is God on Australia side, is God on Ukraine side and so on. And so, it's a critique of the view is that Russia is our enemy.

Vic: What? Was your conclusion?

Michael: For which one?

Vic: The American, is God on America's side?

Michael: No.

Vic: OK.

Michael: He's not, he's not on anybody's side, yeah. The Bible is very unclear as to what side God takes. Most issues we face a today there is a sense of, I guess, an ambiguity. I believe that if it was clear that God was on any one side, it would then mean that the death of someone in war was intentional. God wanted that person to die because I'm on the other person's side. I don't think war works like that. I think that God honors the day that people make decisions in battle, in war and when people die, they die, and they can pray to God. But God isn't really the God that wants us to go around killing each other. He, you know, we are made in his image, and it's not really the intention of God for us to kill each other and war, so, God's not on our side. And this, God bless America stuff, is deeply disturbing. There's no other nation in modern history that's ever really gone down the God bless America mantra, even the strongly Orthodox countries are very careful not to not to tread, so blissfully unaware into the realms of this, God bless whatever country they happen to be. America is in a very dangerous place. I believe this kind of presumptuous expectation that God is on their side it's just pure, pure vanity and everything comes to an end. Vic, what goes up must come down if you want to see the future of America, go to the museum you'll see what happened to empires that think they last forever? Yeah. And the Chau Chuk Wing Museum in University of Sydney is a great museum to see that you see all the samples of all the empires that have come and gone, and it's very humbling because you think, wow, America will go the same way as these countries as these nations and at the time they thought they were invincible.

Vic: The idea that I've heard bantered around a fair bit is that there's two Christian holy lands do in America is 1 and Israel as the other. Can you explain to me why I hear this so much?

Michael: Probably delusional. The Bible doesn't talk about any Holy lands at all, not even the Holy Land is the Holy Land. There's been so much killing there over the last 2000 years, it seems astounding that God would call that holy. There's some Americans there is, there is a school of thought in American theology that believes that they are the seat of God's will for the last days and that the state of Israel is a sign of the end, the beginning of the end.

Vic: Now this is, this is what I've heard and something about the Jew. They need the Jewish people to protect the Holy Land. And then 400 Jews will be saved, and the rest will be slaughtered.

Michael: ...Basic rule of thumb is that if there's any version of Christianity to come out of America, it's probably wrong because they can't for some reason, they can't separate faith and flag. For them, for many of them, not all of them, but for many of them they can't distinguish the fact that faith is personal, it's communal, it's not related to the state, you can be an American and not a Christian, God is not, America is not a Christian country. America is a nation state. Some of its population are followers of Christ. But it's not a Christian state, it's not a Christian nation, never was, never will be. It's not the light on the hill, not the great experiment. And unfortunately, a lot of this American garbage has come into Australia, and you have Australians talking about America is God's country, blah blah blah. What it does, it deletes the history of the Eastern Orthodox completely the Russia, Ukraine, they all have the Eastern Orthodox which they've had for a very long time, the Greek Orthodox, the Syrian Orthodox and the Orthodox in the Middle East and so on, the Coptic Church, you know, the Americans, that version of

Christianity is deleted. And all that matters is our fast-food Jesus, our American hot dog Jesus, our American, you know, white, God Bless America, Jesus, our Trump, Jesus. And it's all just some kind of delusion in a way. I mean, if it wasn't America, if they weren't American, if it wasn't the fact that the Americans were talking about it, I would think that someone was eating a few magic mushrooms actually, because it's so bizarre, it's just so out there, you have the Bible, and they just throw the Bible away and they come up with the bizarre theology. And if you go online, there's these guys who have thousands, hundreds of thousands of subscribers, and all of America's enemies are God's enemies. Everything that America does is for God and is complete and utter rubbish. Yeah, right. And it's a tragedy for people like Biden or whoever wants to be president for the Democratic Party. This is a formidable opposition because these guys are religious zealots, the kind of which sort of make the Taliban sort of pale in significance because they believe Jesus is on their side. This Jesus is the conqueror come to destroy the enemies of America, which are probably hot dogs and fast food, but don't tell them that.

Vic: But that was great. Thank you. And sorry I cut you off. What was the third publication that you wrote.

Michael: The third book was looking at the contest between Diablos and Jesus in *'Is Russia Our Enemy?'* and the fourth book was *'Following Jesus when the Church has* *lost its way.'*

Vic: Right. So that's what you were talking about before?

Michael: Yeah, and my final book What are the pronouns of God? That's coming out coming out next week, probably or the. Week after, OK. Yeah.

Vic: Now, what's the basis of that one?

Michael: It's looking at the identity of Jesus trying to come to terms with what the Bible said is the identity of Jesus is, and I think really the Bible starts with the humanity of Jesus, starts with his human identity and sort of builds from there and so people in the church will automatically say, Jesus is God. They will say, Jesus, the reason he was able to be successful was that he was God. For me that's not how the New Testament reads. The New Testament shows Jesus as a human being because he was a person. And it starts from his humanity and then builds up from his humanity to an understanding of his divinity. And what we in the West have done is we've twisted it around. So, his humanity is kind of seen as inferior or irrelevant. And so, what that does is that effectively makes our lives redundant, and it all becomes about this spiritual experience, whereas Jesus he was a human, he lived our life. And so, by living he, in a sense, sanctifies our experience, our life. And he identifies with us and for me that's an important thing for people. Searching for their identity today identity is a big issue. People don't know who they are. And churches traditionally are saying, you can't be that you can't be this. There's sort of a list the churches have in terms of identity, but Jesus isn't saying that. I don't think the New Testament is saying that at all. I think the New Testament is saying find out who Jesus is, investigate the identity of Jesus, and try to understand him. And in understanding him, you might be able to understand yourself, but the church is wrong where it stands up and says these particular genders are wrong, they're sinful, they're wicked, and you have to be I guess you have to be a certain type of gender you have to be a certain type of color and there is always there's always with these criticisms of gender of this gender debate, there's it's never just gender. And you see slipping in this kind of thinking goes back to what we were talking about with Japan, the reimagined culture. So, what a lot of Christians do is they reimagine the West, and they reimagine it and say we were wonderfully Christian, we had a Christian society when women were women, women within the home, women were given birth, men were working and it's never just about gender. It's kind of promoting this, this idea that as a Christian, you have to be a certain type of person. As a Christian, we follow a certain kind of Savior. That's the difference. And so, the fascists will say, and a lot of Americans are fascists. They say, *'what would Jesus do?'*

have you ever heard that phrase, *'what would Jesus do?'* Yeah, that's not what a Christian would say. A Christian would never say that. A Christian would say, *'what did you Jesus do?'* Well, who was Jesus? That's their question. And so, for Christians, we're interested in the identity of Jesus, the identity of God. We're not interested in what we have to do because we want to understand who he is. And once we understand who God is, then we can everything else, I guess falls into place, and there is freedom, remarkable freedom and that's what the Christian life is about it's about living as free people.

Vic: Do you think it's deliberate that the church has taken the humanity of Jesus and turned it into like some sort of almost fantasy spiritual thing that is beyond what we can do or achieve as humans?

Michael: Absolutely. Yeah. Yeah, so.

Vic: You talk about some of the more human aspects of of Jesus. Because I remember these and they are never really, I went to Sunday school in the 80s and they did talk about it then, but I it's something that I think has slipped from public consciousness. Just what he did and who he cared for. And who he looked out for when he was alive.

Michael: Absolutely. This I think when you look at the life of Jesus, he was someone who treated everyone the same. Yep, he didn't have any favorites, he respected women. He had a great respect for women, he elevated women well above their cultural norms. He spoke to women, which was a no no in those days. Yeah, he crossed the boundaries in terms of religious purity. So, there were rules about uncleanness and being impure before God. You weren't allowed to touch lepers. You weren't allowed to touch the sick. He did all of that. He touched them and he showed for us the model of what a healer is, and then the church says, *'no, no you need to have the Covid passport.'* He also engaged with his enemies. And he conversed with these enemies. And I think he loved his enemies because if you don't love your enemies, why would you talk to them? Why would you engage in conversation with them if you don't care about them or care about where they're going? And so, a lot of the contests he had with the Pharisees were, we say that Jesus hated the Pharisees, or the Pharisees hated Jesus. But those stories are recorded for us to show that we can't ignore the other person who agrees with us. We have to engage not only with those we with whom we agree, but also with those with whom we disagree. That's the Christian approach and love these enemies. He was a very forgiving person and showed the path of forgiveness. And I think for me that these are all things that are so radically different to the way the church is today, and the church has a long list of those who are not allowed to be in. You're either in or you're out and the list is getting longer and longer and longer, and the number of people, the types of people who are not welcome in the church exceeds the types of people who are allowed to go in. And so that's the tragedy because they just don't understand. And Jesus often says, *'you don't understand,'* like he would say something, or he'd do something to his disciples would either say the wrong thing or they do the wrong thing. He would be his response would be, *'you just don't understand.'* And I think that we must say that to the Church today, they just don't understand. And they need to be loved as much as anyone because they're to be pitied, above all, because they're the ones who claim to follow God, and yet they don't want to follow God themselves. So, this is the tension of the of the Christian today. But Jesus is the model, and he's, it's interesting but the Monty Python and the Life of Brian, when they were asked to explain why they chose Brian as the as protagonists, they said, well, we wanted to, to make fun of Jesus. So, we read the New Testament and we thought, well, there's nothing we can make fun of. He actually was a really decent fellow, so we had to come up with something else. So, they came up with Brian and I thought that's really there's more of Christianity in what they said than much of what you can hear in churches today because they understood who Jesus was. He was a man of love, compassion, and kindness.

You know when we were telling you suggested if I still play the shakuhachi? And here we are. I've got it.

Vic: Oh, this is the Japanese bamboo flute.

Michael: Yeah, the Japanese bamboo flute. Yeah.

Vic: Yeah. Yeah, yeah, yeah, yeah. I did ask you. About that, yeah.

Michael: I was, I was gonna play it for you. I'll play it for you next time, Vic.

Vic: Oh no, but I was just gonna ask you before you go. I just. I was fascinated by the fact that when I looked it up online, they were discussing that there's two competing schools and I didn't understand what the concept was behind the school of the Mountain and the School of the Moon and how that's got to do with an instrument. It's just a bit confusing.

Michael: It's like a lot of things in Japan, because if there's a lot of confusion trying to find out truth from reality. I was taught by a teacher by the name of Arakawa Eizan. It refers to a type of mountain and there was a member of the Tozan School and Tozan was started in 1896. The Kinko's school started in the early 1870s. There are some sort of superficial differences. The Tozan school music is in traditional western notation, so you and it's in book form, so it's easy to put on the music stand. But the Kinko school they say, *'we don't do music stands. That's too Western.'* So, they have a scroll. They put on a scroll. So, they always looking down, playing music on the ground. You can't put it on the screen on the stand. The

Kinko school also believes that their ancestry comes from a group of Buddhist monks who were wandering around Japan with a basket on their head playing the shakuhachi called the Komuso monks. There's a sort of myth about this as well and people are still debating, trying to work out what is true and what's fake. I suspect that it's a good story, probably not true. Like a lot of things in Japan a really great story. We do know that the monks were assassins for the government. And so, when the Edo government collapsed in the 1867 revolution, one of the first things they did was to eradicate that version of Buddhism, because those guys were out there hunting, they were killers, basically hired guns for the government, wandering around Japan with their shakuhachi bumping people off.

Vic: So, Hollywood movies are right sometimes.

Michael: They are absolutely right, and I think it's amazing in those movies they have the shukuhachi and you can defend yourself using this bamboo flute against someone with a samurai sword, which is incredible since the samurai sword is the sharpest sword in the world. So, I'm not entirely sure how that's possible in the movies, but the Kinko school is from them. They were both products of the modern era, their ensemble music, it's ensemble music. Basically, the Koto is the other instrument, I think Korea might have a few instruments similar to the Koto and the shamisen, and they play together, so a typical day when we played when I played shakuhachi was we would start at 9:00, would go to someone's house, and we're pretty much nine to five would play a piece that would go over half an hour and then we'll play another piece have some sake, have some food, play a little bit more a few more hours and then go off and have dinner. And it was a wonderful experience and I remember asking my teacher about the about the history and they said look, the shakuhachi is like the clarinet. Clarinet players just loved to play the clarinet. I love to play the shakuhachi. It's an instrument. And if you listen to Aker Bilk or Galway, with the flute, these guys they sort of become one with the instrument and it doesn't have to be a shakuhachi to connect with something spiritual. I think anyone who plays a musical instrument be it a piano, be it jazz or classical, they have this connection with what they're playing. The shakuhachi is just the Japanese version of the clarinet.

Vic: So, when you say that you would sit down and play, from 9:00 to 5:00, what would it be like? A structured kind of day? Would there be conversation?

Michael: One of the funny things about these schools is that in Japan, the idea of a hobby is different to what we understand hobby, so for me, stamp collecting is something I might do once in blue Moon. But in Japan, if you're into stamp collecting, you do every day, every spare moment. With the shakuhachi it is every weekend, and all day so you'd go to these meetings, the concerts would go for hours and hours and hours and there'd be dozens of performances, dozens of pieces. Almost like a marathon in a way, yeah. But they really love their music. And I think for them the music kind of conjures up an image of Japan that is sort of lost in modernity and kind of a world that they want to return to. And I think for a lot of people who play music, regardless of what country they're in, the music sort of elevates their spirit and takes them to a place beyond the everyday. It takes them to kind of a beauty, beauty of the music and that's why people play it with the Koto and the shamisen, so in the Shakuhachi ensemble you play your bit, the Koto players would play their piece the shamisen players would play their piece, shakuhachi players would play our piece, then we'll play together and then its sort of like playing in an orchestra in a way, and very comfortable once you overcome the sitting position, which is incredibly painful, you kind of sit there blissfully for hours.

Vic: And is this associated with Buddhism?

Michael: Again, this is another bone of contention in the literature, having the amongst the followers, the some of the Kinko school would argue that it's connected with Zen Buddhism. Yeah, for but most of the shakuhachi players, they just love the instrument, but for them it's just an instrument. They love playing it. For me when I play it, I really enjoy it. It kind of connects me with Japan, but also it has such a deep resonating tone to it that it kind of elevates you to a different dimension. And so, if you have any shakuhachi players out there who are looking for a musical group let me know. I had a musical group like when I was in America, I played with a, with a pianist and guitarist. We had a little trio going for a while, so if you know of anyone who wants to start a band, let me know.

Vic: it sounds like you're kind of going for meditative state or a trance. That that's fascinating and can you just hold up?

Michael: Yeah, it's a western notation. So, Tozan, who was the one who wrote it, gives you the modern time, which is here 2/2 time. Once you know the notation, and the notes it's a relatively easy but there are many octaves to play and you only have 5 holes and so a lot of it is, I guess your ability to play and to blow into it harder to get the higher notes and so on. It's a demanding instrument, but you can also make shakuhachi from bamboo if you're so inclined as well.

Vic: For you, please, play it now.

Michael: I could play now if you. Like, yeah. Yeah, of course.

Vic: I want to hear what it sounds like. No pressure.

Shakuhachi Music interlude.

Vic: Very fascinating. Thank you so much, Mike. Where I think that I'm excited about your book that's coming out.

Where can people get access to your books. You also do a podcast as well. Where can people find this?

Michael: Freedommatterstoday.com is the website and also the books are available on Amazon and Hidden Road Publishing. The main website has all the links and everything. I'm starting a new podcast mix here probably, which will be more politically oriented. Looking at fascism, tyranny, democracy, politics, culture, economy and trying to be, I guess building some of the more politically controversial areas. So that will be next year. Next year also a few other things, setting up an online store next year for Freedom Matters Today and trying to, I guess branch out into a few new areas, which is exciting.

Vic: I think that if you do you start that podcast the politics podcast next year, I think you could do it very well. You process and speak and articulate at a very, very high level, what are your political economists, professor, priest, and you've got international experience, which is rare as well, it's all there, so I reckon you should really do that. I mean obviously keep going with the books, but I think you're really strong communicator.

Michael: Thank you very much.

12

22 DECEMBER 2023

Interview with Hrvoje Moric, on the "Hrvoje Moric Show," on TNT Radio

https://tntradiolive.podbean.com/e/michael-sutton-on-the-hrvoje-moric-show-22-december-2023/

Topics: Identity of Jesus, new book, meaning of Christmas

TRANSCRIPT

Hrvoje: It's the second hour I'm coming to you from the beach here in Mexico, cartel territory, as I like to call it's we got Michael J Sutton of freedommatterstoday.com coming back on the program. He's out in Australia, he's got, he's published a lot of books, I highly recommend them. I think in the new year, once I get some things settled, I'll be buying probably all of his books in physical form hiddenroadpublishing.com. I think he's self-publishes there on a wide variety of topics, and I always love chatting with him. He's a very cool head, you know, very nuanced. He was in Russia recently. He called in from Russia. And so, we will be talking to him....

Hrvoje: Alright, returning to the broadcast is Michael J. Sutton, political economist, professor, priest, pastor, now a publisher, CEO of Freedom Today, the website freedommatterstoday.com. He's got a podcast, and he also writes for Brownstone Institute, brownstone.org. You can also head over to hiddenroadpublishing.com. He's got a long list of books on a wide variety of subjects there. How are you doing Michael?

Michael: Well, thanks, Hrvoje, and Merry Christmas to you and your family this year. And may you have a happy New Year as well.

Hrvoje: Same to you, perhaps you know one of the few remaining networks TNT radio where we can actually say the C word at Christmas. I had a podcast guest not long ago and during my interview with them I was taken aback because it was the first time in a long time where someone actually said, Common Era instead of, you know, 2000 AD, they said Common Era. And I'm still thinking well, even if you say Common Era, it's still 2023 years after what, you know yeah, any thoughts on that you know this idea of trying to use in the Year of our Lord, or before Christ and use before Common Era.

Michael: It reflects the sort of a cowardice of the culture, really. But I think it also reflects a genuine sense that people don't know who Jesus is. And I think we have to in some ways respect that because one of the great failings of Christianity has been really to convey the identity of Jesus effectively and so we have the, we're coming and celebrating Christmas at the moment and we have little baby Jesus no crying he makes we have all the pomp and pageantry, and in this a lot of people know about Christmas, but they don't really know who Jesus is. And so, part of this frustration on their part, probably part of it, is this, this genuine sense that they have no idea who they are. And they have no idea who God is as well. And so, I think we need to try and meet them where they are and accept their bizarre obsession to eradicate Jesus from history, which is probably the last thing that the people of the 1st century did because they knew exactly who he was because they'd seen him live.

Hrvoje: And I would have thought you know, at least they would try a different avenue, you know it's completely absurd to use the you know, the calendar year as one way to erase Jesus because it's still 2023 years after the Jesus event. You can't get out of that, so I thought that was a weak attempt, but I also got a silly question for you, Michael, is Bruce Willis's *Die Hard* a Christmas movie?

Michael: Well, there's a few answers to that, but I probably couldn't repeat them on air, but probably if you're in a particular way, in particular frame of mind and if you were sitting watching it with, with the mates or people who appreciate that kind of thing. But it certainly was an incredible film when it was first broadcast, it was, it certainly, what was the name of the guy who played the villain? He went on to play Severus Snape in *Harry Potter*. I think it was a much better role, but he was incredible as the evil, evil German villain. A great film, probably a Christmas movie. What do you think Hrvoje?

Hrvoje: I would say so. You know, back when we didn't have the Internet or you know when it was just cable TV, they'd always be playing *Die Hard*, or *Home Alone*, around Christmas time and it's just become at least for me part of that culture. And I don't think it's a bad thing and you know I also in a way treasure whatever, you know whatever people say about Hollywood these days and the bad things that come out of it, I view Bruce Willis as an icon. He's made a lot of, you know, powerful films. He starred in a lot of powerful films that were, you know, good, family movies as well. And yeah. And it's a shame that, you know, his health has just been completely downhill, and I don't know if he's coherent anymore. It might have been the Pentagon juice shot or not. But you know, we all get old, you know Robin Williams died some years ago. And so statistically 10 out of 10 people die. Michael, you know I got, I got that from Ray Comfort of Living Waters, am a big fan of him and 10 out of 10 people die, real quick Michael, we're gonna jump to our headlines and be right back.

Hrvoje: We're back with Michael J. Sutton of freedommatterstoday.com. Also, he contributes to brownstone.org. I love the work that they're doing and Hidden Road Publishing where you can check out his books and we were going to discuss Christmas a bit. Michael, I know, last year around this time, people could check the archives I had as well really great guests to discuss specifically Christmas as people can check the archive, but you know something else, something happened here recently in Mexico which was kind of sad. And in in Mexico it's interesting, a big thing is what we call it the Posadas right, like the get together and family is really big here in Mexico people spend a lot of time with their family. They have these big get-together with big meals, lunches, and dinners, that last like half the day and it's unfortunate because I don't see them this happening so much in the Western world, anymore, like the US or Europe, it's still a big thing in Mexico, which is great. But you know, unfortunate turn of events recently, 12 people died at one of these Christmas gatherings in Mexico. The cartel shot up the party because I think one of the attendees was a rival cartel member. But you know 12 people died attending innocently this Christmas Party, but you know, hey, it happens. And so, your thoughts on how in the Western world these sort of family get togethers are sort of dying and then your wider thoughts on Christmas.

Michael: Yeah, it's a really good observation. I hadn't really thought about it. I think probably the Christmas in Australia has always been sort of a family and friends affair. I think most Australians are fairly relaxed about Christmas. One thing I have noticed in the last few years is the extension of Christmas from the time around the 25th all the way back to almost the beginning of December. And so, we have Christmas events, end of year Christmas parties, Christmas Carol Services. We went to a great Christmas Carol service a few weeks ago, actually down by the beach and hundreds of people, maybe over 1000 people there and they sang all the secular Carol sang some beautiful Christmas carols, Christian songs under the stars under the gum trees, participated, joined by various choirs and so on, and so I think rather than I guess, Christmas becoming more of a secular event, I think it's becoming more of a celebration of human life and about family and about bringing people together. It's also a sense because it ties into New Year as well, it ties into all those very strong European traditions about New Year, about the beginning of a of a new season and in Australia, of course we have a sunny Christmas, we don't have a wintery Christmas, but there it is becoming more of a Christmas of lights, Christmas of celebration and I think these are all very positive things. A time to rest and reflect, but at the same time it is missing the essential element of Christmas because it is a time of Christ, it's the birth of. Christ and it goes back to what I was, what I wrote a book recently called *'What are the pronouns of God?'* And it's my latest book. And it's a critique of identity politics in the West, primarily because people today are very unsure, as I was saying, who they are, where they're going, we want everyone to know who we are. I wrote in the book that 20 years ago for man to say he was a rabbit we would lock him away. These days, we give him a job, we allow him to eat his lettuce and hop around the office and make him the CEO, so people have many different definitions of what it means to be a human being today, some people don't even identify as human beings. And so, I thought, well, what are the, what are the pronouns of God? And for me, the pronouns of God are the exclusive claims of Christianity, that the presence, the power and the person of God is found in the identity of Jesus. And so, for me it's time to pull out the big guns, as they say, and to go back to what the Bible says about who God is and the identity, what the identity of Jesus is, and for me I jump onto the identity bandwagon and say great, you want to talk about identity, let's talk about the identity of God. And from my point of view, we need to understand who Jesus was and what's interesting Hrvoje, is that as I was doing my research on the book, the early Christians took several centuries to work out who they decided Jesus was anyway, because it wasn't until several centuries later that we have the great Declaration of the Athanasian Creed and other creeds but certainly in the New Testament, between AD 30 AD not CE, but you can say CE if you want to, ADCE sounds like a rock band from AD 33 to AD 70, the identity of Jesus is clearly stated in the New Testament and particularly the Book of the letter to the Hebrews, which was written before the fall of Jerusalem. Very contentious claim there but so what we have in the New Testament is that Jesus is both human and that's how the Bible presents him. But through this human Jesus, we see the rise of the Jesus as the Son of God and Jesus identified as the presence of God amongst us, and for me Christmas time is a time where we need to remind ourselves that it isn't little baby Jesus, but we have the presence, the power and the person of God found in Jesus amongst us, and he is amongst us today.

Hrvoje: And what you mentioned is something that for many years now I've thought about, you know, attending,

Christmas events in in in many countries that I've lived in, whether it was in the US or Croatia, Switzerland, Mongolia, Kazakhstan, Mexico, wherever it was celebrated, and often people would celebrate, you know, whether it was at my school where I worked here in Mexico, we'd have Christmas get-togethers and Mexico's more Catholic and so they might have a little bit it might be a little more explicit, Christ. You know, they have different events, they have this big like cake where they throw in like a baby Jesus. And then we would cut it, it would be every person's turn to cut the cake and take the slice. And then if you got the slice with the little baby inside, you would have to pay for lunch for, you know, the entire department or whatever, stuff like this. But I would always think in the back of my mind what you just mentioned that it's Christmas, we're all celebrating Christmas. It's about Jesus, and no one's talking about him. And I would just try to find a way. I think you know to be the one, to put my foot forward. But let's talk about Jesus for a moment and his importance, because we're all here celebrating this event. But no one wants to talk about it because it's politically incorrect, right? And so, you know, any thoughts on that and then and trying to sort of break that silence?

Michael: Yeah, absolutely. I think we need to really go back to the identity of Jesus, which is what I'm trying to do with Freedom Matters Today, talk about the identity of the person, the words of Jesus, his life. And I think for a lot of people who are repelled by the church or repelled by institutional religion, I think the way to open a conversation is to start talking about the authenticity of the life of Jesus. The kind of person he was, his kindness, his love, his generosity, his compassion, his mercy, his forgiveness, and the more we talk about Jesus and his life and the kind of person he was, I think that really resonates with people because people are looking for authenticity. They want something real. And I think that one of the problems of the past, I remember, I grew up with the idea with, I remember a Bishop said to us, *'don't try and understand it, just believe it.'* And for me, I've always had a problem with that because in the New Testament we have the story of Mary, the mother of Jesus, who thought her son was nuts. And there's an episode where she tries to restrain Jesus. And lock him up or lock him away because he was an embarrassment. And so here we have Mary, the mother of Jesus, who was allowed to doubt she's allowed to go on her own journey of discovery. And somewhere between that period and the cross she comes to see him as he sees himself, the Son of God, the Messiah. And so we need to allow people the opportunity to process the identity of Jesus for themselves instead of telling them well, you have to believe you have to believe, we can present to them the account of the New Testament and say to them well, look, you know the New Testament account is a very balanced view of the life of Jesus, Peter and Paul, they reject the extremities. The Gospel writers state things, they don't try to justify events. They just say this miracle occurred and they just write about it, they don't try to, I guess sort of defend it. And so, they're also trying to understand the identity of Jesus. And even at the resurrection of Jesus, a number of the disciples doubted that he rose from the dead, even though he was there amongst them. And so, we have this testimony about him that God wants us to, to encounter Jesus through our own process of investigation to read the New Testament, to come to terms with who Jesus said he was and who he is for us today and I think that's a really important place for people to start, because the Bible presents Jesus as the as the message of God, certainly the letter to the Hebrews is encouraging the Jewish people of the first half of the 1st century to see Jesus as the Messiah and not to go back to the temple and not to go back to the Torah, but to accept Jesus as the Son of God. And what's remarkable about Hebrews is that you have in the first couple of verses, they're all the aspects, the characteristics of Jesus. He is the one who sustains the world through the power of his word. He's the one who achieved the purification of sin, provided the purification of sin. He's the one who is the heir of all things. He's the one through whom the universe was created and so what we've done is we've turned Jesus into little baby Jesus, no crying he makes, we're making him into some kind of emblem for our political ambition, but we're talking about not only the Son of God, but as the letter to the Hebrew says, Jesus is the exact representation of his being. And in Greek, it's the same substance. Jesus is the same substance as God. And so that's why I say that the exclusive claims of Christianity is that the presence, the power and the person of God is found in the identity of Jesus. And the other thing Hrvoje, is that we often talk about the resurrection, and we try to convince people of the resurrection, but I don't think that's really the most important thing. The most important thing is to know who Jesus is, and for the early Christians and the early Jews, the identity of Jesus was the key issue. It wasn't the resurrection, because the idea that someone would rise from the dead, well, it's very common in the ancient world, but the claims of Jesus about his, his divinity and his relationship with his Father were definitely the reasons that got him killed.

Hrvoje: And well, I yeah, I would think resurrection is part of his identity because, you know, he came back and he's alive today. And that is part of that identity and just, you know, one more thing that came to mind is how more and more people and more and more countries, especially the West, they're not using the term Christmas, they're saying, hey, happy holidays are here in New Mexico, they say fiestas happy, sort of like parties, and I always try to respond back: Merry Christmas, particularly, but you know, since you mentioned what he was killed for, you know John Whitehead of rutherford.org, you may be familiar with him. He writes around this time of the year. He always writes an article. And this one was fantastic, called born in a police state, the deep states persecution of its most vulnerable citizens, and he talks about Jesus, he says. *"What if Jesus had been born 2000 years later? What if, instead of being born into the Roman police state Jesus had been born at this moment in time? What kind of reception would Jesus and his family be given? Would we recognize that Christ child's humanity, let alone his divinity, would? What do we treat him any differently than when he was treated by the Roman Empire?"* And he says this, and he gives one example which I think, basically I think he wouldn't have been treated any differently, maybe even worse if you were born in this time. But in any case, I want to get your further thoughts on this and more after the break. It's time for our break. Again, the websites freedommatterstoday.com. You can find Michael's articles that Jeff Tucker's brownstone.org also hiddenroadpublishing.com. Feel free to leave any questions in the chat in my email or call in. We'll be right.

Hrvoje: It's our final segment with Michael J Sutton talking about all things Christmas and you can get his new book, *"What our God's pronouns, the identity of Jesus, from a Christian perspective."* over at Amazon just published a week ago and I was talking about John Whitehead of rutherford.org his great article *"Born in a police state,"* and he talks about if Jesus were born today and he says consider the following if you will. *"Had Jesus been born in the era of the American police state rather than travelling to Bethlehem for a census, Jesus's parents would have been mailed to 28-page American Community Survey, a mandatory government questionnaire, documenting their habits, household inhabitants, work schedule how many toilets are in their home, etc. The penalty for not responding to this invasive survey can go as high as $5000 instead of being born in a manger, Jesus might have been born at home, rather than wise men and shepherds bringing gifts, the baby's parents might have been forced to ward off visits from state social workers intent on prosecuting them for the home birth. One couple in Washington had all three of their children removed after social services objected to the two youngest being birthed in an unassisted home delivery."*

And you get the gist, John Whitehead goes on and on and giving many of these examples. Any thoughts on that? Because you often talk about fascism and freedom and your thoughts on that if Jesus was born today, and you know where we are. It just seems like the tyranny continues to slowly get worse.

Michael: Absolutely Hrvoje. I would say that Jesus was born at home in the Greek it says that there was no room for him in the in the house or in the room. And so it was probably, was that Joseph, went to the family home and because he was a young spouse with his or engaged to be married to Mary, they were not married at that stage, and they were kind of forced to have the worst part of the house, so grandpa, grandma and mum and dad and all the other relatives got the first and second bedroom and they were shoved right at the back. And so that's why they were near the animals because they got the worst position. And I think sort of goes into the humility of the birth of Christ and it shows something that we elevate is something very positive, but at the time it was something very humiliating for them and for Jesus, of course, as he came to understand his role and his relationship with his Father, to submit to his Father's will to do what God wanted him to do, something that the gospels talk about. And we get little glimmers of that throughout the Gospels, Jesus, struggling with his will, struggling with the mission that he'd been given to be the sacrifice for the sin of the world. But that's why he came. He came to restore our relationship with God. He came to be the Savior of the world, to die for sin, as the writer of the letter to the Hebrew says that he provided purification for sin, a statement that would have been deeply offensive to the Jewish hearers of that time, Jesus was not a Levite. He was a descendant of David, which meant nothing in those days, but for him to even assert that Jesus was the one who provided purification for sin in its totality, so the entire sin of the world was paid by his death on the cross, as I often say, Jesus stood where we could not stand, he fought because we could not fight and he died in our place for our sin. But I think also the birth of Jesus is such a wonderful thing, because God decided to reveal himself in human form, and so what God does is he blesses and sanctifies the human experience, that it's a beautiful thing, it's a wonderful thing, human life. The experiences of Jesus were our experiences. He wasn't a real estate magnate like Donald Trump. He didn't play golf, but he did experience our life in its totality, the difficulties and the trials, and so he understands what it means to be human because he himself became human and he did exhibit his divine power only for the benefit of others. He never used his divine power for his own benefit, and his Father in heaven never came to his aid, as he often did to the aid of the Israelites and the Old Testament because he wanted Jesus to live a completely human life and to suffer as we suffered. And so, for me, I think that's another way to talk about the relevance of Jesus for people today, because God is not this distant deity, elusive mystery, but God is a person, in the person of Jesus who came to live our life and to share our suffering, but once he experienced this, he went back to heaven after the resurrection and is seated at the right hand of the Father. And so, there's an elevation to his kingship status that he suffered for us. He died for us. He lived for us. And now he continues to advocate for us before his Father in heaven. And so, for me, Christmas is about celebrating the beauty of life, because God decided to become human and wanted to live our experience. And so, as we celebrate with our friends and our families, we can do so not with the sense that I think the Western Church has sort of made this artificial distinction between the spirit and the flesh, that everything about the flesh is bad, wicked, sinful. There's nothing wrong with a good meal. There's nothing wrong with catching up with friends at museums. Go to Russia, there's hundreds of museums, beautiful art throughout Europe and in America, the creativity of the human spirit, the wonder of the beauty of creation. These are all God's gifts to us Hrvoje. And what the world has said, the West, we're this constant struggle with the Left and the Right and the up and the down. But I think Christmas reminds us that God came, he dwelt amongst us, and the word became flesh and Jesus died for us, so we might live and have life to the full, and so we ought to do that because Jesus has finished his work. And we are to continue his work amongst those who don't know him.

Hrvoje: Well, you just mentioned, kind of reminds me of why I try to always stay focused on the bigger picture you might, you know, people might notice myself as a guest, as a host, I often kind of like always, I'm looking at big, big picture, generally asking my guests because you know a lot of stuff that they're just details and yeah, I always think of eternity, life and death, as you mentioned, God Christ, and judgement. And I don't have time for, you know, this this racist stuff. You know, there's people, conservatives who are obsessed with, like the, the white race being a race. I'm just like, you know at the end of it, I believe there is only one race, I don't personally view that as important and technically always kind of point out I'm not even white, I'm a Slav. Slavs are not really considered white. But you know, all these little squabbles and I'm like, let's put that aside. Let's come together, people from the Left, from the Right. Let's just know unity and you know what, we shouldn't seek unity above all things. You know, there are things that are of doctrinal importance when it comes to Christ and God. But I think we need to spend more time looking at the bigger picture and contemplate death because its coming for us all sooner or later, which is another reason why I'm not so afraid of it, because eventually we're all we're all going to die and any other thoughts on Christmas or New Year's or anything else.

Michael: Well, I think that anyone, I think Hrvoje,

anyone can come to know God. Paul says that there were supporters of the House of Caesar who called themselves Christians. There were supporters of Herod who was a nasty piece of work, but some of the Herodians were Christians, and so even members of the deep state can come to know Jesus as their Lord and Savior. And maybe even, maybe even Donald Trump. Who knows? I mean, no one is beyond the love and mercy of God.

Hrvoje: Or Hulk Hogan. I don't know if you saw this story. 70-yearn-old Hulk Hogan year old WWF just yesterday got baptized.

Michael: OK, so no one is beyond the love and mercy of God, and I think as long as we accept the identity of Jesus and I think through understanding who he is, we can understand more clearly who we are and I think that's a great comfort for many people who are searching for their own identity and don't know who they are, so I think for me, Jesus is the presence, the power and the person of God, and once we know who he is, we can follow him and we have that assurance that we're following the one who went before us and provided that purification for sin. And who enabled us to know the Father again, and so this is not just for us westerners, but for everyone, and I agree with you, Hrvoje, it's not about black or white up or down. We're all in the human race and it's for everyone that God sent Christ and Christ came for everyone, even white people.

Hrvoje: Yeah, and I just continue looking at this this article from John Whitehead. It just really amusing the thought experiment he conducts here where he says, *"Jesus' antigovernment views would have resulted in him being labelled a domestic extremists while travelling from community to community, Jesus might have been reported to government officials as suspicious under the DHS to see something, say something, programs rather than being permitted to live as an itinerant preacher, Jesus might have found himself threatened with arrest for daring to live off the grid or sleeping outside,"* because, you know, in a number of cities that's criminalized now and so really, that and you know, and some there's nothing new under the sun as it's written in, in Ecclesiastes, but also some things have changed in 2000 years. We got 3 minutes to midnight. You know, any other thoughts any thoughts on what may await us on the other side of the New Year in 2024.

Michael: Well, the author to the letter of the Hebrew says we're in the Last Days. He wrote that 2000 years ago. And so, we await the return of Christ. We await the end of all things and new heavens and new Earth. And we're just called to follow Jesus wherever he leads and to know God and to know ourselves, really. And this Christmas time is a time for us to reflect, to celebrate, to be with family and friends and remember that God decided to become one of us and he celebrated our life, so we might celebrate him.

And so, I wish you a very happy, happy, merry Christmas, Hrvoje, to you and your family and to everyone there at TNT radio and thank you for the wonderful opportunity of coming on and talking with you this year.

Hrvoje: It's same to you out there in Australia on the other part of the world. It's just amazing, sometimes this technology that we have, I'm here from the beach in a roving radio host, you're out there in Australia. And again, your book is available on Amazon. It says it's temporarily out of stock, but I'm sure anytime you make an order, you'll get it whenever the stock comes back in and you've got another yet another book as well you just mentioned to me that you're working on, and so any thought on that as well, let us know, all of your projects and places we can find you.

Michael: Yeah, it's Freedom from Fear, freedommatterstoday.com. And so, we have various plans for next year, new projects coming up, all our books are available through Amazon. And we'll go into the e-books next year as well, so you can get a copy Hrvoje, you've inspired us to do that, so thank you for that motivation, but yeah, it's been a wonderful privilege to talk about faith and life and how the Christian faith applies to our existence and our experiences in our crazy world. But I don't think much will change. I think Whitehead's probably right. I think there would have been a lot of, as I say, deep state people who do see themselves as followers of Jesus, as there were Romans who supported the Savior, there's a great blessing too, so not much, not much changes, but God is with us every day, and so God bless.

Hrvoje: All right. I look forward to talking with you next year. Michael freedommatterstoday.com. I'm signing off…Keep on rocking in the not so free world. That's what Jesus did, be seeing you.

ABOUT THE AUTHOR

Michael J. Sutton is the author of eleven books, seven on faith, life, and spirituality, three novels, and one on the politics of demography. He is also the CEO of Freedom Matters Today, looking at freedom from a Christian perspective. For more information, go to freedommatterstoday.com.

www.ingramcontent.com/pod-product-compliance
Lightning Source LLC
Chambersburg PA
CBHW071301110426
42743CB00042B/1133